Your Words Are Your Power

LANG LEAV

Andrews McMeel
PUBLISHING®

6/1/2021

Wrapped up, in you.
In your sweetness.
In your softness.
I live to be consumed by you.

Andrews McMeel Publishing
a division of Andrews McMeel Universal
1130 Walnut Street, Kansas City, Missouri 64106

www.andrewsmcmeel.com

ISBN: 978-1-4494-8716-4

The Fell Types are digitally reproduced by Igino Marini.
www.iginomarini.com

ATTENTION: SCHOOLS AND BUSINESSES
Andrews McMeel books are available at quantity discounts
with bulk purchase for educational, business, or sales
promotional use. For information, please e-mail the Andrews
McMeel Publishing Special Sales Department:
specialsales@amuniversal.com.

The Universe of Us

Also by Lang Leav

Love & Misadventure
Lullabies
Memories

The Universe of Us

LANG LEAV

Andrews McMeel
PUBLISHING®

Andrews McMeel Publishing
a division of Andrews McMeel Universal
1130 Walnut Street, Kansas City, Missouri 64106

www.andrewsmcmeel.com

ISBN: 978-1-4494-8012-7

Library of Congress Control Number: 2016941971

Editor: Patty Rice
Designer, Art Director: Diane Marsh
Production Manager: Cliff Koehler
Production Editor: Erika Kuster

The Fell Types are digitally reproduced by Igino Marini.
www.iginomarini.com

ATTENTION: SCHOOLS AND BUSINESSES
Andrews McMeel books are available at quantity discounts
with bulk purchase for educational, business, or sales
promotional use. For information, please e-mail the Andrews
McMeel Publishing Special Sales Department:
specialsales@amuniversal.com.

For Michael, my universe.

INTRODUCTION

Magic tumbled from her pretty lips and when she spoke the language of the universe—the stars sighed in unison.
—MICHAEL FAUDET

I believe we think more deeply about the universe when we're falling in love. I think the mysterious pull that draws you to another person is identical to the one that moves our eyes upward to the stars.

The Universe of Us is my fourth book. As a child, I always loved the romance of the night sky. While writing this new body of work, I revisited that sense of wonder and fascination that I have held as far back as I can remember. The sentiment can be best described as a mixture of nostalgia and longing.

In many ways, a book is, in itself, a tiny universe. Each page is like a newly formed galaxy, fashioned from a single, pulsing thought. A book travels for days, for years, sometimes for centuries to meet you at an exact point in time.

I hope you enjoy *The Universe of Us* as much as I have enjoyed putting it together. I like to think it has found you for a reason, even if that reason is only to draw your eyes skyward once more.

Much love,
Lang

We drift from star to star,
your soul and mine
as one.

We fall nearer to the moon—
we fly closer to the sun.

How We Began

It was how we began. Your mouth against mine, your fingers tracing along the back of my neck.

You asked me to imagine what it must have been like, for the first two people who fell in love; before the word *love* was conceived.

You said it felt like that for you. Like we existed in a time before love—as though we were waiting for the word to catch up to the feeling.

What I Would Tell You

To you, love was about multitudes.
To me, love was inordinate.

> *I love you*, I would say.
> *How much?* you would ask.

I couldn't find the words to answer you then. But they have found their way to me since. And this is what I would tell you.

I would blanket the world in utter darkness; I would pull back the veil of light and reveal to you a blinding crescendo of stars.

I would drain all the seven seas and ask you to count—one by one—every grain of sand that clings to the ocean floor.

I would tally the beat of every human heart that has echoed since the dawn of our becoming.

And as you look in awe at the sheer magnitude of my admission, I would take your hand in mine and tell you; if only you had let me, this is how much I could have loved you.

DISTANCE

It was all I wanted for the longest time—to open my eyes and see you there. To stretch out my hand and touch the soft, yielding warmth of your skin. But now I have learned the secret of distance. Now I know being close to you was never about the proximity.

I Loved Him

I loved how his eyes danced merrily,
    and the gentle way he spoke;
    the way he filled my aimless days,
    with bitterness and hope.

I loved him as I fell to sleep,
    and each morning as I woke;
    I loved him with all my wayward heart—
    until the day it broke.

FIRST SNOW

I fell in love on the third kiss, the first snow, the last slow dance. Ask me what day we met and I can only smile and shake my head. It could have been a Tuesday or the death anniversary of a beloved monarch and I wouldn't have a clue. Our love story comes to me in waves, in movie stills and long summer afternoons spent under a sky of incessant blue. I still think of your eyes in flashes of color, your hands in a frenetic, feverish blur—your smile a mosaic of light and shadow. I still find myself lost in those moments of abstraction.

A POSTCARD

To the man I love, to my future.

The first time I felt your presence, I began joining the dots in the sky, wondering when our stars would align.

I often think of where you are and if you're happy. Are you in love? I hope she is gentle. I know you and I are the same in that way—we bruise a little more easily than most. You see, our souls were made in the same breath.

I know I'm running late—I'm sorry. Things haven't worked out the way I planned. But believe me when I tell you I am on my way.

Until then, think of me, dream of me and I will do the same. One day I will learn your name, and I will write it somewhere on this page. And we will realize that we have known each other all along.

RECOGNITION

I've never met you before, but I recognize this feeling.

SOMEONE LIKE YOU

Do you think there is the possibility of you and I? In this lifetime, is that too much to hope for? There is something so delicate about this time, so fragile. And if nothing ever comes of it, at least I have known this feeling, this wonderful sense of optimism. It is something I can always keep close to me—to draw from in my darkest hour like a ray of unspent sunshine. No matter what happens next, I will always be glad to know there is someone like you in the world.

To Know Him

If you want to know his heart, pay close attention to what angers him.

If you want to know his mind, listen for the words that linger in his silence.

If you want to know his soul, look at where his eyes are when you catch him smiling.

YOUR LIFE

You've wandered off too far,
    you've forgotten who you are;
    you've let down the ones you love,
    you've given up too much.

You once made a deal with time,
    but it's slipping by too fast;
    you can't borrow from the future,
    to make up for the past.

You forsake all that you hold dear,
    for a dream that is not your own;
    you would rather live a lie—
    than live your life alone.

I Am

He said loving me was like seeing the ocean for the first time. Watching the waves crash senselessly against the rocks, over and over. Grabbing fistfuls of sand as it trickled through his fingers, like my hair, brittle as ebony, strong and taut like the bumps of his knuckles. He said it was like swallowing his first mouthful of the sea—the sudden shock of betrayal.

He said loving me was like panning for gold. Sifting through arsenic, waist-deep in toil. Lured by the shimmer and promise of transcendence, like the river between my lips, a floodgate that opens for him—only when I choose.

And I told him, if I am so hard to love, then let me run wild. My love is not a testament to my surrender. I will show you just how much I love you, with the inward draw of every breath— the collective sigh of the world and all its despair. But I will never give you what you want in chains.

CHOOSE LOVE

My mother once said to me there are two kinds of men you'll meet. The first will give you the life you want and the second will give you the love you desire. If you're one of the lucky few, you will find both in the one person. But if you ever find yourself having to choose between the two, then always choose love.

TODAY

Today I am not in my skin. My body cannot contain me. I am spilling out and over, like a rogue wave on the shore. Today I can't keep myself from feeling like I don't have a friend in the world. And no matter how hard I try, I can't seem to pick myself up off the floor. My demons are lying in wait, they are grinning in the shadows, their polished fangs glinting, knowing today, it will be an easy kill. But tomorrow, tomorrow could be different, and that is what keeps me going today.

The Butterfly Effect

Close your eyes and think about that boy. Tell me how he makes you feel. Let your mind trace over his tired shoulders. Allow your thoughts to linger on that beautiful smile. Take a deep breath and try to put those dark thoughts aside. For once let go of the reins you've wrapped so tightly around your heart. I know you are scared. Who could blame you? Love is a hurricane wrapped inside a chrysalis. And you are a girl walking into the storm.

IMPOSSIBILITY

Do you know the feeling when you're so happy that you can't imagine ever being sad again? Or when you're so sad that you no longer believe you could ever be happy? When you tell me you love me, I always think of that strange emotion—that feeling of impossibility. You say you love me, and you can't imagine a future without me in it, yet all I can think of is how you must have felt the same way once about someone else.

SHOOTING STARS

I want to light a spark tonight, without striking up a memory
of you. Please don't send me shooting stars when my mind is
a loaded pistol.

PROCESSION

He used to ask me all the time if I was okay. As though he never knew for sure. He would ask me when he was tired or frustrated or when he felt helpless. He would ask me when he was afraid.

He asked me that same question, long after we stopped being lovers—when we became something less yet somehow more. *Are you okay?* He would whisper on the phone late at night, when his girlfriend was asleep or had gone to her mother's for the weekend. *Are you okay?*

He hasn't asked me in years, but I know he still thinks it. I know the question still reverberates in his mind like a broken record and he will keep looking for answers long after there is nothing left to appease him.

It was always the same question, over and over again. Like the start of a procession. And it took me years to recognize the unsaid words that marched silently behind.

Are you okay; *because I love you.*
Are you okay; *because I need you.*
Are you okay; *because I don't know how to live without you.*

THE LONGEST GOOD-BYE

The longest good-bye is always the hardest. Love for the sake of love is the most painful of all protraction.

MOMENTS

That's the tragedy of growing up—knowing you'll run out of feeling something new for the first time. The sad thing is you only get so many of those moments—a handful if you're lucky—and then you spend the rest of your life turning them over in your head.

I think that's why you meant as much to me as you did, why I held on for so long. I didn't know it back then, but you were the last time I would ever feel anything new.

MOMENT OF TRUTH

One day I looked at you and it occurred to me how beautiful
your smile was. I heard music in your laughter—I saw poetry
in your words. You asked me why I had that look on my
face, as though a shadow had fallen across its sun-drenched
landscape, heavy with premonition, dark with revelation.
The second I tried to tell myself I wasn't in love was the
moment I realized I was.

STILL

We may not be in love anymore, but you're still the only one who knows me.

CONVERSATIONS

"Most people want to save the entire world. It's a lovely thought, and I'm not saying it's not a noble pursuit—but it's impossible to save everyone. You just have to pick your little corner of the world and focus your energy there. That's the only way you will ever make a difference."

"But I don't know if I can make a difference. It feels like I am screaming at the top of my lungs, but no one can hear me. No one cares. How can I change anything if I'm completely powerless?"

"You may be powerless now, but there will be a time when you won't be. Don't you see? And that's the time for you to be loud, to tell the world about the changes you want to see, to set them in motion."

THE LAST TIME

When was the last time you said I love you and meant it. When was the last time you heard those words back.

When was the last time you felt like someone knew you and not the person you've been pretending to be. When was the last time you felt like yourself.

When was the last time you heard someone say his name. When was the last time it killed you to hear it.

When was the last time you felt love well up in you like a newly struck spring. Like an outpouring of the soul.

When was the last time he called you beautiful. When was the first.

A LESSON

There is a girl who smiles all the time,
    to show the world that she is fine.

A boy who surrounds himself with friends,
    wishes that his life would end.

For those that say they never knew—
    the saddest leave the least of clues.

SAHARA

And the weather was so damn sick of being predictable; I heard it began snowing in the Sahara and I wanted to tell you that I've changed.

AFTERMATH

I want to talk about the aftermath of love,
    not the honeymoon or the hitherto;
    but the upshot and the convalescence,
    the slow, hard hauling—the heavy tow.

I want to tell you about those evenings,
    that crept inside like a vagrant cat;
    and cast around its drawn out shadow,
    untoward—insufferably black.

I want to write about the mornings,
    the sterility of the stark, cold light;
    struck against a pair of bare shoulders,
    the lurid whisper of a misspent night.

I want to convey the afternoon setting,
    the water torture of the sink;
    drip by drip, the clock and its ticking,
    and too much time left now to think.

CROSSROADS

It was a quiet love, a tacit love. It came without prelude or preamble. We never said the word *love*—we didn't have to. It was in our laughter, in the sense of wonder we found in each other. And if we had doubts then, time has told us otherwise.

It was a gentle love, a tactile love. It was all hands and lips and hearts in tandem. There was motion in our bodies and emotion in our discourse. We were a symphony of melody and melancholy. When you find peace in another's presence, there is no mistaking.

It was a kind love, a selfless love. I was a dreamer, and you were a traveler. We met at the crossroads. I saw love in your smile, and I recognized it for the first time in my life. But you had a plane to catch, and I was already home.

POSSIBILITY OF LOVE

Yes, I think it is entirely possible to fall in love with someone you've never met. Physicality is an expression of intimacy—not an indication of it.

DARK MATTER

If you know love like I know love when it is full and ready—
like the pulse knows the tip of the blade before the cut—the
blood rushing to greet its serrated edge. You would know love
like I have if you have seen the sun in every possible gradation
of light; if you can hear the birdsong beyond the rudimentary
call—if you can distinguish between each cadence as it quivers
through the air. If you get so cold sometimes that it burns or
the heat gets so bad your teeth start to chatter—then you will
open up your arms and take this dark thing into the fold and
you will know love like I know love.

FOR THE WORLD

I talk to you all the time, even if you can't hear me. I tell
you constantly, over and over, how much I miss you and that
for me, nothing has changed. I think about the days when
we could say anything to each other. My heart is like a time
capsule—it keeps safe the memory of you. I know it's harder
with you gone than if you had never been here at all—but I
wouldn't have missed it for the world.

A WINTER LOVE

We were like
    the raging sea,
    a winter love
    that could not be.

Our voices were
    the ocean's roar,
    we cried until
    we could cry no more.

We mocked the storms
    and they fell the trees,
    our broken limbs
    among scattered leaves.

The tides had shown
    what we did not heed,
    the water holds—
    and then recedes.

HER TIME

She has been feeling it for awhile—that sense of awakening. There is a gentle rage simmering inside her, and it is getting stronger by the day. She will hold it close to her—she will nurture it and let it grow. She won't let anyone take it away from her. It is her rocket fuel and finally, she is going places. She can feel it down to her very core—this is her time. She will not only climb mountains—she will move them too.

THE CHAOS OF LOVE

I have walked through the ruins of an empire as it fell through the passageway of time. I have witnessed star after star exploding like fireworks, as I fixed my gaze light-years into the sky. And I was only a pinprick of dust on the day they split the atom. I had yet to learn the most destructive thing in the world is the quiet yearning between two people who long to find their way back to each other.

ANYTHING ELSE

I want to plant a seed in your mind, some tiny particle of thought that bears a remnant of me. So little by little, day by day, you find yourself thinking of me, until one morning, you will wake up and realize you can't think of anything else.

Know Me

I remember when I met you
    the hands of time stood still;
    you and your camera smile—
    a flash of something real.

We talked until the evening,
    the moon came out for awhile;
    the clock resumed its ticking
    and my heart was on the dial.

The morning came to claim you,
    and as far as I can tell—
    there will never be another,
    who will know me quite as well.

WHEN

When did you stop caring? he asked.
When did you start noticing? she replied.

A FIELD OF FLOWERS

He spoke to her once about a field of flowers and a warm spring day. He, with his thoughts spilled onto paper, and she, with a sketchbook and pencil in hand. And she pictured them there, with her head on his shoulder and his hand resting on her thigh. She heard the contented chatter of birds and the slow, rhythmic hum of bees. If she could describe happiness to you, it would be that vision he conjured up for her. If she could take from all the possibilities, that moment would be the one she would bring into fruition. And yet the world spins too quickly and it turns too slowly as she waits and waits for the dream to transact into memory. Until the day comes when she can no longer tell the difference.

UNTIL IT'S GONE

"Some people don't know what they have until it's gone."

"But what about the ones who do know? The ones who never took a damn thing for granted? Who tried their hardest to hold on, yet could only look on helplessly while they lost the thing they loved the most.

"Isn't it so much worse for them?"

THE ONE

I don't want you to love me because I'm good for you, because I say and do all the right things. Because I am everything you have been looking for.

I want to be the one that you didn't see coming. The one who gets under your skin. Who makes you unsteady. Who makes you question everything you have ever believed about love. Who makes you feel reckless and out of control. The one you are infuriatingly and inexplicably drawn to.

I don't want to be the one who tucks you into bed—I want to be the reason why you can't sleep at night.

JUPITER'S MOON

I had a dream last night where you and I were standing on the surface of Jupiter's moon. We ascended weightless and free, our bodies no longer tethered to the rules of gravity.

Take my hand and come with me. Let's go to Callisto. Our feet will never have to touch the ground.

LOVER'S PARADOX

Tell me that story again—the one where the world ends how it began with a boy who loves a girl and a girl who loves a boy. And she is deaf and he is blind and he tells her he loves her over and over and she writes him every day but never hears a thing back.

ALL I WANT

I'm not asking for a grand declaration of love. I've stopped entertaining those thoughts long ago. You see, I have resigned myself to where I am now, hanging by a thin, tenuous thread. I can feel it twisting above me, gently fraying, slowly giving way. I'm not asking for promises or tenure—I just want a hand to reach for at the breaking point.

THE REDWOOD TREE

My father once told me a story about an old redwood tree—how she stood tall and proud—her sprawling limbs clothed in emerald green. With a smile, he described her as a mere sapling, sheltered by her elders and basking in the safety of the warm, dappled light. But as this tree grew taller, she found herself at the mercy of the cruel wind and the vicious rain. Together, they tore relentlessly at her pretty boughs, until she felt as though her heart would split in two.

After a long, thoughtful pause, my father turned to me and said, "My daughter, one day the same thing will happen to you. And when that time comes, remember the redwood tree. Do not worry about the cruel wind or the vicious rain—but do as that tree did and just keep growing."

A WHOLE UNIVERSE

The days catapult before me. The world is spinning too quickly. It gets harder and harder to retrace my steps. To figure out how I got to be here.

The years expand into eons. It gets easier for me to imagine my mother as a girl. To think about her worn-out heart— breaking for the things she couldn't hold on to. And I wonder if I've let the wrong people go. When you lose a person, a whole universe goes along with them.

Sometimes I picture all my other selves, standing in line like a row of dominoes; separate but part of the same disjointed whole. How can I hold a single one accountable? No one ever walks away from love, knowing they can never go back.

HEROES

I was never one to believe in superheroes. I always thought they belonged solely within the pages of a book. Until the day one showed up in my life and changed my point of view.

Like some fairy-tale knight, he turned up when I needed him the most. He pulled me out of the mire with his big, strong arms and for the first time in awhile, I felt solid ground beneath my feet. I was as unsteady as a newborn—it was as though my legs had forgotten the simple task of walking. And I clung to him like he was the second coming, and I was the world's newest convert.

I think he hung up his cape a long time ago. I can signal my torch against the window or send a flare up into the sky, and it wouldn't make a difference. No one is coming to save me this time. I guess I'll just have to save myself.

Epiphany

Here are the words that have brought me to a new understanding. Here are the words that will bind us forever. From this day forward, I will speak your name with gratitude, knowing it is the mantra of my soul. I will let you go, knowing we are eternal. We were born to walk this world in intersecting lines. We are circles and signposts and parallels. I have left markers for you at every turn. Look for me in everything that catches your breath. Let the simple miracle of your own presence overwhelm you. For you are beautiful, in ways that can't be described. And we are love at its most inexplicable. With these words, I am one with divinity. With these words, I am one with you.

ODE TO WRITERS

The greatest plight
 of one who writes
 is the irrational fear,
 that what they write
 possibly won't—
 ever be quite as good
 as what they wrote.

GONE

"The sad thing is," she said, "the moment you start to miss someone, it means they're already gone."

AN INSOMNIAC'S DREAM

I missed you today. Between waking and sleeping, I thought of you.

We met somewhere inside an insomniac's dream, in a world so precarious—it could crumble at any given time—folding at the slightest touch.

I wish I could have a day with you, where the sun never went past noon. Or a night, where the stars could go on forming their constellations; until the sky was filled with stories of how I loved you.

You once told me that you had to bend time and space to be at my side. But it would only be for a moment, you had said.

How long? I asked.

But it was already over, long before the answer could leave your lips.

ONCE

I loved you once and now I must spend my whole life explaining why.

Too Much

Are you like me? Do you give too much, too quickly? Do you throw yourself blindly at the world, thinking that it will always open its arms up to you?

Do you feel the slow turning beneath your feet, the shifting plates? Do you sense the streams of fissures roaring underneath like unrequited love, desperate for somewhere to go?

Do you feel the wind pulling back and forth, constricting and expanding, a perpetual cycle as vicious as it is tender, like when it hurts you to breathe but it's the only thing that sustains you?

Are you like me? Do you live with the dial turned up at full volume? Can you taste the salt of the sea when you're miles inland and the ocean feels like a fractured memory?

Are you like me? Are you alive or just pretending?

DARK THOUGHTS

My idle hands
    and restless mind—
    into darkness,
    begin to delve.

Seldom do I think of you,
    but today I thought
    of little else.

AWAKE

I was loved in my dreams last night. It echoed through me like thunder—I felt it through and through.

When I woke up, I couldn't shake the feeling of his arms around me and the sound of his voice, already half forgotten.

The loss was indescribable. And I couldn't help that feeling of certainty that I have felt this way before. Somewhere in time, throughout the ages, I was loved—I was loved and my eyes were wide open.

HER LOVE LETTERS

The truth is there are pieces of me in everything I have written to you, for you. After all, what is a poet but a composite of her love letters?

I WILL CRY

Tomorrow I'll cry for all the world,
    for all the things gone wrong;
    I will cry for every tethered bird,
    who has lost her joyful song.

Tomorrow I'll cry for every heart,
    that has broken, like boughs, in two,
    but today, my love, you have my tears—
    today I will cry for you.

SALVE

"You've made your choice, and there's nothing I can do," she said. "I don't think you want me in your life anymore, and I have to find a way to live with that. You said you would still be there for me, but I don't want to be a mere courtesy—a salve for your guilt. You won't hear from me again after today, and I don't want you to worry. I'll be okay. Because I have to be."

TIME STANDS STILL

In cemeteries
    of memories
    our love will lie
    in caskets.

My time with he
    an eternity—
    neither present
    nor future
    can past it.

My heart still kept
        where it was left—
        if ever he were
        to ask it.

TERRITORY

I think there is a sense of ownership in knowing, isn't there? You let people in, and they claim parts of you—they fly their flag over uncharted territory and from then onward—you cease to belong wholly to yourself.

A PREMONITION

There are some people who you look at, and you can just tell how their story will end. I don't know what it is; they have everything going for them, yet it will never be enough. But when I look at you, I just know instinctively, that despite the odds against you and although life will always find a way to test you, someday you'll have everything you want. Your ending will be a happy one.

NINE LIVES

Does the past ever appear before you, like a bolt in the blue? Something or someone from many lives ago. It knocks you right off your feet, just when you thought you'd found solid ground. But it's only an illusion, isn't it? All this time, the plates have been shifting beneath you and the world keeps spinning round and round like the plates in a circus act. Yet you still can't leave it behind; that one thing that was kept from you. No matter what you are given, it still scratches at the corner of your mind, like a cat begging to be let in.

BLUE

You begin to invent things after awhile. I suppose it's only human nature to add and subtract from our memories; to recall them the way we feel they should be remembered. After all, our lives are a living work of art—shouldn't we be allowed to shape it in any way we choose?

I remember the first time I saw my favorite painting, how its fragile beauty caught my breath. And I thought if the artist had painted just one brushstroke less, he could have told an entirely different story. If he began with a smear of red instead of blue, it could have been a chapter instead of an era.

SELF-LOVE

Once when I was running,
from all that haunted me;
to the dark I was succumbing—
to what hurt unbearably.

Searching for the one thing,
that would set my sad soul free.

In time I stumbled upon it,
an inner calm and peace;
and now I am beginning,
to see and to believe,
in who I am becoming—
and all I've yet to be.

THE EDGE OF THE WORLD

You think falling in love is about holding on, but it isn't. It is about hands gripping the edge of the world and letting go, one finger at a time.

Take a deep breath—here comes the drop. I know it's your first time here, but soon you will get used to the motion; the headlong dive into the deep. Just go with it. You only get one chance to fall in love with your heart still whole.

THE LONELIEST PLACE

I believe there is penance in yearning. There is poverty in giving away too much of your heart. When the desire for another is not returned in equal measure—nothing in the world could compensate for the shortfall. Sometimes the loneliest place to be is in love.

A BEAUTIFUL COLLISION

There was a feeling of inevitability when I met you. The sense that we would be together; that there would be a moment when you would look at me in a certain way, and we would cross the threshold from friendship into something so much more.

We spoke once about lovers who kept finding each other, no matter how many times the world came between them. And I think I had to break your heart, and you had to break mine. How else could we know the worth of what we were given?

I think you were always meant to know me a little better than anyone else. And our lives were fated to converge like some cosmic dance. I know there is a terrible distance between us. But our bodies are made of stardust, and we are hurtling through space and time, toward the most beautiful collision.

HEART AND MIND

Do you think the mind answers to the heart? The way it keeps conjuring up what is no longer there. When in love, we swing like a pendulum between the two. We want the mirage knowing it will never be enough. But the heart does not have eyes and the mind cannot resist when it asks, *tell me just one more time.*

WANDERING STAR

She walks the earth freely, yet her feet never touch the ground. Many hands will reach for her, but she cannot be anchored. She belongs to no one, to nothing, to nowhere. When you meet her, you will recognize her for who she is—a free spirit, a wandering star. She will fit in your arms like she was made to be there. And she will show you what it means to hold something you can never hold on to.

WITHIN MY REACH

I wish the love
    I have come to meet,
    was not an inch
    within my reach.

I wish the prize
    was so far-flung,
    that I would not cry
    if it were not won.

I wish the dream
    was placed so high
    that my panicked heart—
    would dare not try.

QUIET

I've grown quiet now. You won't hear me talk about you anymore. It doesn't hurt like it used to. I suppose that is something to be thankful for.

I will never be the girl I was before I knew you. On some days, I miss her, more than I miss you. After all, she was the one you fell desperately in love with, even if you didn't know it at the time.

You've grown quiet too. I don't think it's for a lack of things to say. Sometimes, things don't work out the way we plan. What's the point in dwelling on what could have been?

I went to sleep last night, thinking about you. Life is just a dream after all. Come and find me when you wake up.

ALL I ASK

Life: a question,
    death: its reply—
    a tender good-bye.

Stay 'til our present
    slips into the past—
    it is all that I ask.

Torn

Some days I feel like my soul is being pulled in one direction
and my heart in another.

Loving You

Loving you is like being ten years old again, scaling a tree with my eyes bright and skyward, wanting only to get higher and higher, without a thought of how I would get back down.

WHAT I HOPE FOR

I am hoping for a sign in the sky or a word from the stars. I am praying for a tear in the fabric of time so you and I can slip quietly away and not a single soul would think to miss us.

THE WEATHER

It was raining on the day I met him—hair wet and tangled—droplets of water sliding down my cheeks like crystal teardrops. He says he can taste sunlight on my skin whenever cherries are in season. With me, he doesn't think about permanence or possession. He knows I'm just like the weather—I'll keep changing my mind.

CRYING

You're still crying about him aren't you? Silly girl. What good will it do you to spill those sky blue tears? You meant either everything to him or absolutely nothing at all.

DARK ROOM

Tell someone about me. I can't bear to think that I have vanished from your world completely. I can't stand the thought of resting like a silent tomb in your heart, shut away from the light. I don't want to be an inscription on the first page of your book or the opening of a trilogy. Have you forgotten everything we spoke about? Could you live the rest of your life without speaking my name?

Tell someone about me; even if it hurts. You once told me that everyone has a dark room. Is that where you have put me? Do my photographs still hang on tenuous cords that twist into your memory?

Tell someone about me. Don't let me fade away like a Polaroid. Time can be cruel in that way. But you and I are still living and breathing in this imperfect world. What could be a greater miracle than that?

Tell someone about me. I don't want our story to end here, and your words may be the only thing that can save us. Relinquish your pride for just one moment—put an end to this interminable silence and tell someone about me. Or tell the whole world.

ORIGAMI

He says that I am ivory and indifference. My eyes are cold and hard like sapphires but behind their wintry gaze, there is a murmur of a girl. He takes my trembling hands in his and tells me I am safe with him. His touch is sweet like a memory of something long gone and I want to fold myself into his arms like origami. He says that I am paper, lily-white, and he will spoil me with words if I let him.

Solace

When all I desired
    was once promised
    to me.

And all have conspired
    to keep it
    from reach.

There is safety in numbness—
    there is solace
    in sleep.

CONTACT

It was the longest she had gone without human contact; without the soft, conceding warmth of someone else's skin. She began to crave it after awhile, to obsess over the most trivial things. Like a hand on her shoulder or a kind word from a stranger. How long, she wonders, before I forget how it feels to be wanted? How long until I lose all recollection of love?

MY HEARTACHE

If this is my heartache, then let it be mine to endure. Permit me to feel it in its entirety. Don't tell me how much of you I am allowed to love.

HANSEL

A feast upon
    I feasted on
    when my eyes
    first looked at you.
    While deep inside
    as I looked on,
    a hunger grew
    and grew.

The time we spent
    came and went,
    as you slipped
    from me
    like hours.

Now I seek of you,
    a speck of you,
    left for me
    to devour.

The crumbs you threw,
    the trails to you,
    I believed they led—
    were in my head.

The crumbs you threw,
    will make me ill—
    yet they are all,
    I have of you.

The banquet done,
    for all but one,
    as the crumbs
    grow fewer and few.

My love will flow
    on and on,
    while slowly
    I am starved of you.

ONE DAY

One day she began talking to him again. After seven long years of silence, there it was, her voice on the other end of the phone, soft and lilting. She had one of those voices that reminded him of a wormhole. The power it possessed to close all that time and distance between them, the way it brought her back to him once more—tenuous and shimmering—like a dewdrop catching the sun.

THE ESSENCE

I saw a swaying tree,
    I felt it sway in me.

A bird trilled out her song,
    To me this song belongs.

What's given is not gone—
    in something it lives on.

THE GIRL SHE WAS

She doesn't feel like herself. Not anymore. She was different once.

Now she is like a watered-down version, pale and thin. She slips through the cracks unnoticed. She fades into the background, afraid of saying the wrong thing. She grows sharp edges and won't let anyone get close to her.

She doesn't know how she came to be like this, how she ended up here. She only remembers the way she used to be—wild and reckless. Bold and unapologetic.

Your Words

Remember, your words are your power. Never forget your words.

4000 MILES

The lines stitched into highways,
    the never-ending seams;
    on roads that are less traveled,
    dividing you and me.

I wish I could unravel
    the fabric in-between,
    and tear away the distance,
    to bring you close to me.

TALK AGAIN

I want us to talk again—the way we used to when the sun was coming up, and we were miles away from anywhere.

I want us to talk again—about all the things we would think about, yet never thought to say out loud to anyone else.

I want us to talk again—like the way we did before we wanted to do anything more than that. I want us to talk.

And if we never talk again, I want you to know that I miss that most of all—and every time the sun goes down, I think of all the things I wish I could tell you.

Breaking Up

You think it happens when you've stopped caring. When all the tenderness and warmth are stripped away and all that's left is cold and empty and broken.

But you never imagine it will happen like this. With our arms around each other, our hearts full of love and neither of us wanting to be the first to let go.

ONE THING

She looked up at the sky and whispered, take anything away from me, take it all if you want to; but please—please just let me keep this one thing.

CHASING BUTTERFLIES

She flitted in and out of his life like a recurring dream. Even when she was an arm's length away—it felt like she was somewhere else. He would reach out and touch her and his hand would come away empty.

AND THEN

I always thought the words *and then* were a prelude to something wonderful. Like seeing a ship come in or finding a note in your letterbox, when you weren't expecting one. That swift, surprising transition from nothing to everything.

And then.

Two little words that hold a world of promise.

And then the light pierced through the dark, forbidding sky, and the rain stopped falling.

And then I met you.

Jump

"Don't you get it?" he said. "The ones who are afraid of heights don't trust themselves enough not to jump."

LONELINESS

I don't know when I last caught myself staring at the clock.
It must have been before the hour hand began turning for
somebody else. Since then I have become a deft collector of
minutes, like a caged bird hungry for the sky. Do you know
I have thoughts that could color all the oceans blue? Those
who harbor dreams of being alone must have forgotten what
loneliness is.

Punished

"We were happy," she said, and her eyes, downcast and brimming, reminded him of how the sky was before the first splash of rain. "We were happy and they punished us for it."

CIRCLES

My mind, a Venn diagram.
　　You, the overlap and the intersect;
　　a pulsating glimmer—omnipresent,
　　a lighthouse with its glowing breath.

You are the stone that skirts the river,
　　that skips along its crystal plane;
　　a surface skimmed by concentric shimmer,
　　and trembles with the touch of rain.

You are worlds that spin in orbit,
　　a star who rose and fell;
　　infinity summoned for audit—
　　a penny toss in the wishing well.

CONTRITION

There was a look in his eyes I had never seen before. And it took me a few moments to recognize it for what it was. *Remorse.*

I don't deserve you, he said, half-defeated, half-hopeful. It was the most honest thing he had ever said to me. And he was right. He didn't deserve me. Not by a long shot. But he had me nonetheless.

Your Darkest Self

I think love is about being your darkest, most destructive self.
To be loved, not in spite of this but because of it.

COLLISION COURSE

Tomorrow I will tell you that I love you. Nothing in the world can stop the maddening rush of those three words. *I love you.* I know you were born with your heart already broken. But the world began in pieces and somehow made itself whole.

Tell me where to put the stars. Show me how the oceans keep spilling over. Your smile is a blazing trail of light, shot down from the heavens. And I know how much this is going to hurt. But it's too late for me to get off this collision course. Tomorrow I will tell you that I love you. And nothing in the world can stop the maddening rush of those three words.

HE

He is the thought behind the feeling,
    the swelling in my chest;
    the starlight in the evening,
    the yearning when I undress.

He is the sound behind the sighing,
    the song of every bird;
    the tears in all my crying,
    the ache in every word.

PREDESTINED STARS

He and I collided like two predestined stars and in that brief
moment I felt what it was like to be immortal.

Key Turn

There we were at the breaking point when you told me you could explain everything if I would just let you. But I wouldn't. That was the moment I chose to pull the door between us firmly shut.

I always wonder what you would have said if I had let you continue. Perhaps there was something in your explanation that would have allowed me to trust you again—that would have made sense of it all. As unlikely as that scenario could have been, my mind remains firmly hinged on the possibility—the key turn of a chance that maybe, I had it wrong all this time.

THE PERFECT CRIME

It wasn't with knives
    my heart he tore;
    when he brought me
    to death's door.

It wasn't his hands
    that had me slain—
    but he had killed me
    all the same.

Cold and callous
    with no remorse,
    he turned me to
    a walking corpse.

And I am imprisoned
    in this pain,
    while he without
    the slightest blame—
    free to do it
    over again.

WAR ON LOVE

Write about the first thing that comes to your mind; that your heart has longed to remind you. Write about the thrumming rhythm that implicates you—the lingering thoughts that tempt you. Write about the one thing that absolves you.

Write about the peace you've found in denial—the salvage in walking away. It's okay; no one blames you. You can't wage war on love if you don't know your limits.

Eros

If time were governed by Eros, I would stay in your arms forever. If time answered only to lovers, I would never leave your side. The seconds pass by slower when I'm staring at the clock. And you wonder why I can't take my eyes off you.

A BOOKSTORE

Standing in a bookstore, near a street where you used to live, I found myself wishing you would walk through the door and we would meet for the first time—all over again.

THE PIANO

Love was never meant to be black and white. But I knew the truth could free me as my hands were poised over the keys and I could have made them sing, I could have made them sing, but the feeling went away and I lost the courage to tell you.

STITCHES AND SCARS

We all want to be on par,
    to steal the wish
    from someone's star.

Our flaws and failings
    stitches and scars,
    to be loved
    for who we are.

REMORSE

You loved her and now you know what you've lost. Now your hands feel emptier than before you met her—your heart feels heavier. But you were young and you were careless. How were you to know the value of what you were given?

Yet a part of you did know. In some strange, mysterious way, you knew there was something special about that girl. In her eyes, you caught a glimpse of your own destiny. You knew it was meant to travel with hers.

If only you could go back to that day; to the one where she stood before you, gentle and hopeful—waiting for you to make up your mind. When you had thought to yourself that nothing could ever look as beautiful.

That was the moment you should have told her what your heart was telling you. If you had allowed it, she could have been your whole world. All you had to do was open the door. All you had to say was, *come in.*

RAVINE

I think maybe we were cursed or just plain unlucky. You had your ideas about love, and I had mine. And as much as we tried, we couldn't make it work. I don't think it was the lack of feeling or intention that broke us—it was one small misunderstanding after another. Isn't it strange how a minor disparity can grow into a ravine? In the end, it was enough to tear us apart.

YOUNG LOVE

Screeching tires, a near miss. A horn blaring sharply into the night. I close my eyes. Here come the flashbacks.

We were losing track of the days and nights, counting fireflies and waiting for the sun to come around. I was so addicted to you. I remember the exquisite fatigue as I fought off sleep for another hit—another line of conversation. We drove down freeways and winding roads, in a sleepless stupor, the stereo blasting love songs that were a cheap imitation of what we were feeling. Sometimes I wished you would take us over the edge, and we would be forever young and crazy in love. Go slow around those curves. I only want you safe now. It doesn't matter if we're together or apart. I love you so much. I'll love you, right until the end.

ACKNOWLEDGMENTS

I would like to thank Al Zuckerman and Samantha Wekstein from Writers House for their continued guidance and support.

To Kirsty and her team at Andrews McMeel for their hard work and dedication.

To Oliver Faudet, one of the brightest stars in my universe.

To my family and friends, I am so lucky to have you in my life.

And a very special thank-you to my readers. Your support means the world to me.

About the Author

Lang Leav is the international best-selling author of *Love & Misadventure*, *Lullabies*, and *Memories*. She is the winner of a Qantas Spirit of Youth Award and coveted Churchill Fellowship. Her book *Lullabies* was the 2014 winner of the Goodreads Choice award for poetry.

Lang has been featured in various publications including *The Straits Times*, *The Guardian*, and *The New York Times*. She currently resides in New Zealand with her partner and fellow author, Michael Faudet, in a little house by the sea.

INDEX

Join Lang Leav on the following:

Facebook   Tumblr   Twitter   Instagram

Lullabies

Also by Lang Leav

Love & Misadventure
Memories
The Universe of Us

Lullabies

Written & Illustrated by
LANG LEAV

Andrews McMeel
PUBLISHING®

Andrews McMeel Publishing
a division of Andrews McMeel Universal
1130 Walnut Street, Kansas City, Missouri 64106

www.andrewsmcmeel.com

ISBN: 978-1-4494-6107-2

Library of Congress Control Number: 2014941351

*The Fell Types are digitally reproduced by Igino Marini.
www.iginomarini.com*

ATTENTION: SCHOOLS AND BUSINESSES
Andrews McMeel books are available at quantity discounts
with bulk purchase for educational, business, or sales
promotional use. For information, please e-mail the
Andrews McMeel Publishing Special Sales Department:
specialsales@amuniversal.com.

For Michael

I love you, I do—
you have my word.

You have all
my words.

CONTENTS

INTRODUCTION

"A mind possessed by unmade books."

This line, taken from the poem *Lost Words* by Michael Faudet, illustrates my lifelong preoccupation with books. All artists have a motive, a passion that wills them to create the things they do. For me, it has always been about books. It always will be.

It was from a very young age that I fell in love with this wonderful artifact—the turn of the first page is almost like a sacred ritual to me. Whenever I walk into a library, it is never without some degree of reverence.

Over time, my love of books spilled beyond the joy of reading and I began to dream of books filled with my own words and pictures.

This dream turned to reality with the publication of my first book, *Love & Misadventure*, and continues now with the follow-up, *Lullabies*, the very book you are holding in your hands.

I have always thought poems were a little like spells—incantations that are as old as time. There is a certain quality to words that—when strung in a certain way—has an almost hypnotic effect. This combined with the universal theme of love, becomes ever more potent and intoxicating. After all, what greater magic is there than love?

I hope you enjoy reading *Lullabies* as much as I enjoyed putting it together. I imagine it to be a bedside table kind of book—hopefully, one that you will pick up on some windy, restless night and it will help sing you to sleep.

Though it has a start, middle, and end, you can begin reading *Lullabies* from any page you wish. Some pieces will sing to your present, others may echo of your past, and the rest could whisper of your future. Remember, while the words on these pages remain static, this book—like all other books—is a living and breathing thing. Much like a mirror reflecting its ever-changing landscape, *Lullabies* is a book that, over time, will reveal itself to you slowly.

Much Love,
Lang

Lost Words

A midnight scribble,
    a morning sigh;
    you watch the words
    curl up and die.

Madness lives
    inside your head,
    of poems lost
    and pages dead.

A mind possessed
    by unmade books,
    unwritten lines
    on empty hooks.

    —Michael Faudet

Chapter 1

In books unread,
we lie between
their pages.

As they turn us to lovers
like season's changes.

—EXCERPT

HER WORDS

Love a girl who writes
    and live her many lives;
    you have yet to find her,
    beneath her words of guise.

Kiss her blue-inked fingers,
    forgive the pens they marked.
    The stain of your lips upon her—
    the one she can't discard.

Forget her tattered memories,
    or the pages others took;
    you are her ever after—
    the hero of her book.

My Heart

Perhaps I never loved enough,
    If only I'd loved much more;
    I would not nearly had so much,
    left waiting, for you in store.

If I had given away my heart—
    to those who came before;
    it would be safer left in parts—
    but now you have it all.

Metamorphosis

I am somebody else's story. The girl who served their drink, the person they pushed past on a crowded street, the one who broke their heart. I have happened in so many places, to so many people—the essence of me lives on in these nuances, these moments.

Yet never have I been bolder or brighter than I am with you. Not once have I ever felt so alive. Whatever vessel we pour ourselves into, mine is now overflowing, brimming with life. It is transcending into something new.

Hands are no longer hands. They are caresses. Mouths are no longer mouths. They are kisses. My name is no longer a name, it is a call. And love is no longer love—love is you.

When

When every dream
   has turned to dust,
   and your highest hopes
   no longer soar.

When places you
   once yearned to see,
   grow further away
   on distant shores.

When every night
   you close your eyes,
   and long inside
   for something more.

Remember this
   and only this,
   if nothing else
   you can recall—

There was a life
   a girl once led,
   where you were loved
   the most of all.

Tsunamis

Be careful about giving your heart too quickly, I was told.
Boys only have one thing on their minds, they cautioned.

I don't know if he truly loves me—how can I be sure? I can't say with any conviction that he won't break my heart—but how could I have stopped him from taking what was already his?

He swept in like a tsunami, wave after wave, and I didn't stand a chance. All those warnings, all the things they tried to prepare me for—lost in an instant—to the enormity of what I felt.

Thoughts of You

There were times when I was with him and it was too much. Does that make sense? When someone stirs a world of emotion in you and it's so intense you can barely stand to be with him.

During those moments, I wanted so desperately to leave—to go home, walk into my bedroom, and shut the door behind me. Crawl into bed and lay there in the dark, tracing the outline of my lips with my fingers—replaying everything he said, everything we did. I wanted to be left alone—with nothing other than my thoughts of him.

He's Leaving

My nine
    is your noon;

            I'm just packing now—

your winter,
    my June.

            wish I could pack you.

PATIENCE

Patience and Love agreed to meet at a set time and place; beneath the twenty-third tree in the olive orchard. Patience arrived promptly and waited. She checked her watch every so often but still, there was no sign of Love.

Was it the twenty-third tree or the fifty-sixth? She wondered and decided to check, just in case. As she made her way over to the fifty-sixth tree, Love arrived at twenty-three, where Patience was noticeably absent.

Love waited and waited before deciding he must have the wrong tree and perhaps it was another where they were supposed to meet.

Meanwhile, Patience had arrived at the fifty-sixth tree, where Love was still nowhere to be seen.

Both begin to drift aimlessly around the olive orchard, almost meeting but never do.

Finally, Patience, who was feeling lost and resigned, found herself beneath the same tree where she began. She stood there for barely a minute when there was a tap on her shoulder.

It was Love.

. . . .

"Where are you?" She asked. "I have been searching all my life."
"Stop looking for me," Love replied, "and I will find you."

Passing Time

I feel the end is drawing near,
    would time be so kind to slow?
    You are everything to me, my dear,
    you are all I really know.

But as I sit and wait and fear
    and watch the hours go—

Everything that happened here
    happened long ago.

No Other

There is someone I keep in my heart—I love him and no one else. It is a love that will only die with me.

You may ask, *death could be some time away—what if from now to then, you love someone new?*

Well I can tell you, there is only one love. If any person claims to have loved twice in all their life—they have not loved at all.

WELL WISHES

My love, are you well,
    past the sea and the swell,
    out in the world, where danger is fraught.

Amidst the doom and the gloom,
    and the hospital rooms,
    where hearts can be bartered and bought.

There are words to betray
    and the things that we say,
    can sometimes be snappy and short.

Where the strangers we meet,
    take us down one way streets,
    and forgetting is something we're taught.

Where earthquakes will reign,
    between terror and planes—
    and colds are so easily caught.

Sad Things

Why do you write sad things? he asked. *When I am here, when I love you.*

Because someday, in one way or another, you will be taken from me or I you. It is inevitable. But please understand; from the moment I met you, I stopped writing for the past. I no longer write for the present. When I write sad things, I am writing for the future.

A Pilgrimage

Always seeking,
    each moment fleeting;
    this is where
    my soul will rest.

With you I've fulfilled,
    our destined meeting;
    my tired hand,
    against your chest.

This is the heart,
    that keeps mine beating—
    these are the eyes
    that mine know best.

Loving You

I saw him the other day. His arms around another girl, his eyes when met with mine—were slow in their recognition.

I wonder if he remembers what I once told him.

I will love you forever.

He had smiled at me sadly before giving his reply.

But I am so afraid you may one day stop.

Now all these years later, I am the one who is afraid. Because I love him, I still do. I haven't stopped. I don't think I can. I don't think I ever will.

And/Or

I once wrote a book and called it *And/Or*. It was about choosing between either, or having the option of both.

I'm not sure why I wrote it. Perhaps it had something to do with how I looked at life. My lack of care. My indecision. I wanted everything because I didn't want anything enough.

Then I met you and it changed me. For once in my life, there was something I wanted. So much.

For me, that was the death of the word, *or;* because now, there is no other. It was the end of the word, *and;* for I love only you.

DEVOTION

He is more to me
    than I.

I love him more
    than I can bear.

So much at times
    I wish to die,
    so I can end this
    on a high.

His Kiss

He has me at his every whim;
　　everything starts with him.

To all the boys I used to kiss—
　　everything stops with his.

Us

I love him and he loves me.

We spend every moment together. When sleep parts us, we often meet in our dreams.

I like to take naps throughout the day. *Like a cat*, he says. He is a cat person.

He thinks my eyes are beautiful and strange. He has never seen eyes like mine up close before.

He says they look at him with daggers when he has done something wrong. Like when he forgets to order olives on my half of the pizza.

He thinks I am especially cute when angry.

We argue over whose turn it is to put the DVD in the player. Sometimes no one wins and we end up watching bad TV. Which is never really a bad thing.

He never imagined he would be with someone like me.

Now, he says, he can't imagine himself with anyone else.

. . . .

We're kids, aren't we?
Yes, kids with grown-up powers.

SIGNPOSTS

What if certain people were signposts in your life? Representa-
tions of good or bad. Like an old friend you see across a crowded
street, one you wave hello to, before hurrying on. The last time
you saw them, things took a turn for the worse and, as sad as it
may seem, they have unwittingly become an omen—a precursor
of bad luck.

Or that one person whom you rarely speak with, who can always
be found right where you left them. You carry their smile with
you like a talisman—for whatever reason, their presence in your
life will always bring the promise of better days.

Then there is the boy you can never stop thinking about. When-
ever you see his name, it trips you up. Even if it's one that belongs
to many others, even if he belongs to someone else.

You know he is a symbol of your weakness, your Kryptonite.
How he rushes in like wildfire and burns through everything you
worked so hard to build since he last left you in ashes.

So you do the only thing you know how—you put as many miles
as you can between him. As many roadblocks and traffic lights as
you can gather. Then you build a bold red stop sign right on your
doorstep, knowing all the stop signs in the world could never
hold him—they can only ask him to stay awhile.

Mementos

You were none,
     and now you're all;
     your worth will rise,
     the more I fall.

Like these mementos
     we have stored,
     once were things—
     now so much more.

Keys

Hearts don't have locks, she said.

Some do, he replies. There are people who give away the key to theirs for safekeeping. Others are mistrustful and give out several keys, just in case. Then there are those who have misplaced them but never cared to look.

What about your heart, she asked.

He smiled.

Your words are the key to mine, he replied.

Never forget your words.

Déjà Vu

I saw it once,
    I have no doubt;
    but now can't place
    its whereabouts.

I try to think it,
    time and time;
    but what it is,
    won't come to mind.

A word, a scent—
    a feeling, past.
    It will not show,
    though much I've asked.

And when it comes,
    I soon forget—
    this is how it felt,
    when we first met.

Clocks

Here in time,
    you are mine;
    my heart has not
    sung louder.

I do not know
    why I love you so—
    the clock knows not
    its hour.

Yet it is clear,
    to all that's here,
    that time is told
    by seeing.

Even though
    clocks do not know,
    it is the reason
    for their being.

Lullabies

I barely know you, she says, voice heavy with sleep. I don't know your favorite color or how you like your coffee. What keeps you up at night or the lullabies that sing you to sleep. I don't know a thing about the first girl you loved, why you stopped loving her or why you still do.

I don't know how many millions of cells you are made of and if they have any idea they are part of something so beautiful and unimaginably perfect.

I may not have a clue about any of these things, but this—she places her hand on his chest—*this* I know.

Message in a Bottle

No one truly knows who they are, he sighs. The glass bottle does not know its own contents. It has no idea whether it is a vessel for the most delicious apple cider, a lovingly crafted wine, or a bitter poison. People are the same. Yet like the bottle, we are transparent. We can't see ourselves the way others see us.

How do you see me? she asked.

You are a bottle floating out at sea, he says. One that contains a very important message. It may never reach its recipient, but as long as there is someone waiting, it will always have purpose.

Will you wait for mine?

I will, he promised. I will look for you every time I stand at the edge of the ocean.

You

There are people I will never know
        and their lives will still ensue;
        those that could have loved me so
        and I'll never wonder who.

Of all the things to come and go,
        there is no one else like you.

The things I never think about—
        and the only thing I do.

More than Love

Love was cruel,
    as I stood proud;
    he showed me you
    and I was bowed.

He deftly dealt
    his swiftest blow—
    I fell further than,
    I was meant to go.

And he ashamed,
    of what he'd caused,
    knew from then,
    that I was yours.

That he, an echo
    and you, the sound—
    I loved you more
    than love allowed.

Second Chances

The path from you extending,
    I could not see its course—
    or the closer to you I was getting,
    the further from you I'd walked.

For I was moving in a circle,
    not a line as I had thought—
    the steps I took away from you,
    were taking me towards.

A Phone Call

We said hello at half past one,
    all our chores for the morning done;
    and as we spoke about our day,
    the world began to fall away.

To our highest hopes and deepest fears,
    if I had one wish, I'd wish you here,
    the tantrums and the horror shows,
    the stories only you would know.

All the while with the ticking clock,
    laughing as if we'd never stop;
    we said good night at half past ten—
    at midnight we said good night again.

ENTWINED

There is a line
    I'm yet to sever —
    it goes from me
    to you.

There was a time
    you swore forever,
    and I am captive
    to its pull.

If you were kind,
    you'd cut the tether—
    but I must ask you
    to be cruel.

Stay

The words I heard
      from you today,
      are said when
      there's nothing
      left to say.

What I would give
      to make you stay,

I would give it
      all away.

The Seventh Sea

The answer is yes, always yes. I cannot deny you anything you ask. I will not let you bear the agony of not knowing.

Yes I love you, I swear it. On every grain of salt in the ocean—on all my tears. I found you when I reached the seventh sea, just as I had stopped looking.

It seems a lifetime ago that I began searching for you.

A lifetime of pain and sorrow. Of disappointment and missed opportunities.

All I had hoped for. All the things I can never get back.

When I am with you, I want for nothing.

Over My Head

I count his breaths,
    in hours unslept,
    against hours of him,
    I have left.

With him lying there,
    with him unaware,
    I am out of my depth.

If My Life Were a Day

You are the moment before the sun sinks into the horizon. The transient light—the ephemeral hues set against the fading, fading sky.

Until I am left only with the moon to refract your light. And in your absence, the stars to guide me—like a cosmic runway— steadily into the dark.

*She was different from anything
he had ever known.*

——THE PROFESSOR

Chapter 2

Interlude

Nostalgia

Do you remember our first day? The fog lifted and all around us were trees linking hands, like children playing.

Our first night, when you stood by the door, conflicted, as I sat there with my knees tucked under my chin, and smiling.

Then rainbows arching over and the most beautiful sunsets I have ever seen.

How the wind howls as the sea whispers, *I miss you.*

Come back to me.

The Professor

A streak of light flashes across the sky. Thick heavy raindrops pound the uneven dirt floor, littered with dried leaves and twigs. She follows closely behind him, clutching an odd contraption—a rectangular device attached with a long, squiggly, antenna. "You were right about the storm, Professor!" she yells over the howling wind. "Yes, my assistant!" he cries, voice charged with excitement, as he holds up the long, metal conductor. She stumbles over a log as he reaches out to catch her.

They tumble on the dry grass laughing. He tosses aside the bent, silver coat hanger, wrapping his arms around her waist. The little transistor radio falls from her hands.

The sun peeks through the treetops.

She thinks of their first conversation. "I live by a forest," he said, describing it in such a way that when she came to scale those crooked, winding stairs, it was like she had seen it a thousand times before. As if it had always been there, waiting to welcome her. Like the pretty, sunlit room that remained unfurnished, sitting empty in his house, now filled with her paints and brushes.

She would fondly call him her Frankenstein, this man who was a patchwork of all the things she had ever longed for. He gave her such gifts—not the kind that were put in boxes, but the sort that filled her with imagination, breathing indescribable happiness into her life. One day, he built her a greenhouse. "So you can create your little monstrous plants," he explained.

He showed her how to catch the stray butterflies that fluttered from their elusive neighbors, who were rumored to farm them for cosmetic use. She would listen in morbid fascination as he described how the helpless insects were cruelly dismembered, before their fragile wings were crushed and ground into a fine powder. "Your lips would look beautiful, painted with butterfly wings," he would tease her.

"Never!" she'd cry, alarmed.

They spent much of their days alone, in their peaceful sanctuary, apart from the little visitor who came on weekends. When the weather was good, the three of them would venture out, past the worn jetty and picnic on their little beach. He would watch them proudly, marveling at the startling contrast between the two things he loved most in the world. His son with hair of spun gold, playing at his favorite rock pool and chattering animatedly in his singsong voice. She, with a small, amused smile on her tiny lips, raven hair tousled by the sea wind. She was different from anything he had ever known.

The Dinner Guest

The wine, sipped too quickly, has gone to my head. I watch the way your hands move as you tell your joke and laugh a little too loudly when you deliver the punch line.

His eyes flash at me from across the table. The same disapproving look he shot me earlier, as I was getting dressed.

It's a bit tight.

Don't be ridiculous, I say.

How do you know him, again?

Just an old friend. We worked together years ago.

He clears his throat, breaking my reverie. My grin fades into a small, restrained smile.

You top up his glass.

The conversation drifts into stocks and bonds. My mind begins to wander, like a bored schoolgirl.

Your hand brushes my leg.

Was it an accident? I look at you questioningly, but you are staring straight ahead, engrossed in conversation.

Then there it is again. Very deliberately, resting on my knee.

Oh, your hands.

They slide up my thigh and under my skirt, lightly skimming the fabric of my panties.

It's been so long.

I part my legs under the table.

The conversation turns to politics.

A mirror effect, you say.

He looks confused. What's this about mirrors?

The word sends a jolt through my body.

Your hand slips into my panties.

Vania

Vania Zouravliov, *that's* his name! My favorite artist. I wanted his book that time . . . very badly, in fact. I tipped my little coin purse upside down and counted all my money. I was short twenty dollars!

She lies on her stomach by the fire with her sketchpad open, lazy pencil strokes lining the paper with each flick of her wrist.

Oh, poor you, he says sympathetically. Do you know what, sweetheart, we'll get you that book.

Thanks, baby. She smiles at him then returns to her sketching.

I'll tell you how, he continues, snapping his laptop shut.

She looks up, bemused. Pencil down, chin propped in hand. *I'm list-en-ing,* she says in a singsong voice.

Okay, so here's what you do. You go into the bookstore and you buy a cheap paperback novel. Smile sweetly and make small talk with the people at the register. Turn on the charm, *just* like the way you do when you're trying to flog me your sketches. "Hey look! I just drew these. What do you think? D'you wanna buy them?"

She giggles.

Then, he says, after you've finished paying, wander over to where the book is, pick it up and flip through it, looking as if you didn't have a care in the world.

He lets out a small chuckle, leaning forward.

Then my dear, you get as close as you can to the entrance without attracting any attention. *And... you bolt!* As fast as you can, down the escape route that we would have planned the day before. I'll be in the car waiting so as soon as you jump in, I'll put my foot down, *hard,* on the accelerator, speed off to somewhere quiet before we stop and I'll look at you and say, Can you believe you did that? How does it feel? And you'll be sitting there, your adrenaline pumping, your heart racing, hugging the book against your chest, saying, "Oh my God! I *can't* believe I just did that!" Then do you know what I'd do?

What—would—you—do? she says between peals of laughter.

I'd take you out, *fuck* you up against the car.

Dumplings

Her impatient hands work slowly.

Like this, she says.

Then you dip your finger in the egg yolk.

Put it between the sheet and press it down firmly.

She watches as he fumbles.

The little pocket of pastry is foreign in his hands.

She reaches out, placing hers on either side of his face. Pulling
him towards her, she kisses him warmly.

This is why I love you.

The sides of his face are white from her flour-coated hands.

It makes her laugh.

If only you could see yourself the way I do.

He smiles sheepishly.

Yours are so pretty, he says.

He puts down the oddly shaped dumpling.

And picks up another sheet of pastry.

The Garden

The curtain, a smoky gray color, drops from the creamy white ceiling. Crawling with strange bugs and eight-legged creatures, from where an ominous fan whirs.

His hand reaches for the cord. A string of shiny, black beads that glisten against the bright, early evening sun.

Flashback to the time he found her in the garden. White cotton dress pulled up around her thighs, feet blackened by the rich, lush earth that she had just been turning. With an apologetic smile that said, I couldn't help myself.

That Night

It was one of those nights that you are not altogether sure really did happen. There are no photographs, no receipts, no scrawled journal entries.

Just the memory sitting in my mind, like a half-blown dandelion, waiting to be fractured, dismembered. Waiting to disintegrate into nothing.

As I close my eyes, the pictures play like a blurry montage. I can see us driving for hours, until the street signs grew less familiar—the flickering lamplights giving away to stars. Then sitting across from you in that quiet, little Italian place. Your hands pushing the plates aside, reaching across for mine.

The conversations we had about everything and nothing. And kissing you. How I remember that.

It was one of those nights that my mind still can't be sure of. That wonders if I was ever there at all. Yet in my heart, it is as though I've never left.

They gave us years,
though many ago;
the spring cries tears—
the winter, snow.

——MELANCHOLY SKIES

Chapter 3

Finale

THREE QUESTIONS

What was it like to love him? asked Gratitude.
It was like being exhumed, I answered. And brought to life in a flash of brilliance.

What was it like to be loved in return? asked Joy.
It was like being seen after a perpetual darkness, I replied. To be heard after a lifetime of silence.

What was it like to lose him? asked Sorrow.
There was a long pause before I responded:

It was like hearing every good-bye ever said to me—said all at once.

ACCEPTANCE

There are things I miss
    that I shouldn't,
    and those I don't
    that I should.

Sometimes we want
    what we couldn't—
    sometimes we love
    who we could.

Fading Polaroid

My eyes were the first to forget. The face I once cradled between my hands, now a blur. And your voice is slowly drifting from my memory, like a fading polaroid. But the way I felt is still crystal clear. Like it was yesterday.

There are philosophers who claim the past, present, and future all exist at the one time. And the way I have felt, the way I feel—that bittersweet ache between wanting and having—is evidence of their theory.

I felt you before I knew you and I still feel you now. And in that brief moment between—wrapped in your arms thinking, *how lucky I am, how lucky I am, how lucky I am*—

How lucky I was.

Thoughts

Dawn turns to day,
    as stars are dispersed;
    wherever I lay,
    I think of you first.

The sun has arisen,
    the sky, a sad blue.
    I quietly listen—
    the wind sings of you.

The thoughts we each keep,
    that are closest to heart,
    we think as we sleep—
    and you're always my last.

Dyslexia

There were letters I wrote you that I gave up sending, long before I stopped writing. I don't remember their contents, but I can recall with absolute clarity, your name scrawled across the pages. I could never quite contain you to those messy sheets of blue ink. I could not stop you from overtaking everything else.

I wrote your name over and over—on scraps of paper, in books and on the back of my wrists. I carved it like sacred markings into trees and the tops of my thighs. Years went by and the scars have vanished, but the sting has not left me. Sometimes when I read a book, parts will lift from the pages in an anagram of your name. Like a code to remind me it's not over. Like dyslexia in reverse.

Dead Poets

Her poetry is written on the ghost of trees, whispered on the lips of lovers.

As a little girl, she would drift in and out of libraries filled with dead poets and their musky scent. She held them in her hands and breathed them in——wanting so much to be part of their world.

It wasn't long before Emily began speaking to her, then Sylvia and Katherine; their voices rang in unison, haunting and beautiful. They told her one day her poetry would be written on the ghost of trees and whispered on the lips of lovers.

But it would come at a price.

There isn't a thing I would not gladly give, she thought, to join my idols on those dusty shelves. To be immortal.

As if reading her mind, the voices of the dead poets cried out in alarm and warned her about the greatest heartache of all——how every stroke of pen thereafter would open the same wound over and over again.

What is the cause of such great heartache? She asked. They heard the keen anticipation in her voice and were sorry for her.

The greatest heartache comes from loving another soul, they said, beyond reason, beyond doubt, with no hope of salvation.

It was on her sixteenth birthday that she first fell in love. With a boy who brought her red roses and white lies. When he broke her heart, she cried for days.

Then hopeful, she sat with a pen in her hand, poised over the blank white sheet, but it refused to draw blood.

Many birthdays came and went.

One by one, she loved them and just as easily, they were lost to her. Somewhere amidst the carnations and forget-me-nots, between the lilacs and mistletoe—she slowly learned about love. Little by little, her heart bloomed into a bouquet of hope and ecstasy, of tenderness and betrayal.

Then she met you, and you brought her dandelions each day, so she would never want for wishes. She looked deep into your eyes and saw the very best of herself reflected back.

And she loved you, beyond reason, beyond doubt, and with no hope of salvation.

When she felt your love slipping away from her, she knelt at the altar, before all the great poets—and she begged. She no longer cared for poetry or immortality, she only wanted you.

But all the dead poets could do was look on, helpless and resigned while everything she had ever wished for came true in the cruelest possible way.

She learned too late that poets are among the damned, cursed to commiserate over their loss, to reach with outstretched hands— hands that will never know the weight of what they seek.

Time

You were the one
    I wanted most
    to stay.

But time could not
    be kept at bay.

The more it goes,
    the more it's gone—
    the more it takes away.

Broken Hearts

I know you've lost someone and it hurts. You may have lost them suddenly, unexpectedly. Or perhaps you began losing pieces of them until one day, there was nothing left. You may have known them all your life or you may have barely known them at all. Either way, it is irrelevant—you cannot control the depth of a wound another inflicts upon you.

Which is why I am not here to tell you tomorrow will be a new day. That the sun will go on shining. Or there are plenty of fish in the sea. What I will tell you is this; it's okay to be hurting as much as you are. What you are feeling is not only completely valid but necessary—because it makes you so much more human. And though I can't promise it will get better any time soon, I can tell you that it will—eventually. For now, all you can do is take your time. Take all the time you need.

Wounded

A bruise is tender
 but does not last,
 it leaves me as
 I always was.

But a wound I take
 much more to heart,
 for a scar will always
 leave its mark.

And if you should ask
 which one you are,
 my answer is—
 you are a scar.

DESPONDENCY

There was a girl named Despondency, who loved a boy named Altruistic, and he loved her in return.

She adored books and he could not read, so they spent most of their time wandering through worlds together and in doing so, lived many lives.

One day, they read the last book there was and decided they would write their own. It was a beautiful tale set against a harsh desert with a prince named Mirage as the hero. From their wild imaginings, an intricate plot of adventure and tragedy unfolded.

Altruistic awoke one night to find Despondency sitting at her desk, furiously scribbling away in their book. It caught him by surprise for until now, she had not written a single word without him.

Despondency turned to face him, her eyes cast downward. She told him while writing their story, she had fallen desperately in love with Prince Mirage and wanted to wander the desert in search of him.

Altruistic was heartbroken but knew it was in Despondency's nature to long for what she couldn't have, just like it was in his not to stand in her way. Crying, she begged him to burn the tale of Prince Mirage, but he could not bring himself to do it.

They said their good-byes and she asked him if he would carry their book with him always. He promised he would and with one final look, she was swallowed by the swirling desert sands. He knew he would never see her again.

Epilogue

The girl was standing in the graveyard by her father's tombstone when a tall stranger approached. Handing her a worn, leather-bound book, he said, "Your father wanted you to have this." She knew at once it was the book he had carried in his breast pocket, close to his heart for all his life. Her father's inability to read was also something she had inherited, and while tracing her fingers over the cover of the book, she asked, "Can you please tell me what the title is?"

"Grief." the stranger replied.

For You

Here are the things I want for you.

I want you to be happy. I want someone else to know the warmth of your smile, to feel the way I did when I was in your presence.

I want you to know how happy you once made me and though you really did hurt me, in the end, I was better for it. I don't know if what we had was love, but if it wasn't, I hope never to fall in love. Because of you, I know I am too fragile to bear it.

I want you to remember my lips beneath your fingers and how you told me things you never told another soul. I want you to know that I have kept sacred, everything you had entrusted in me and I always will.

Finally, I want you to know how sorry I am for pushing you away when I had only meant to bring you closer. And if I ever felt like home to you, it was because you were safe with me. I want you to know that most of all.

Always with Me

Your love I once surrendered,
    has never left my mind.

My heart is just as tender,
    as the day I called you mine.

I did not take you with me,
    but you were never left behind.

Love's Inception

I did not know
    that it was love
    until I knew.

There was never
    another to compare
    with you.

But since you left,
    each boy I meet,
    will always have you
    to compete.

Karma

Sorrow tells stories,
    I relay them to wisdom;
    I play them like records
    to those who will listen.

I know to be thankful,
    I was given my time;
    to those who have loved him—
    your heartache is mine.

To the one who will keep him,
    and the hearts he has kept
    your love, when it leaves him—
    his greatest regret.

Fairy Tales

When she was a little girl, she went to the school library asking for books about princesses.
You've read every book we have about princesses.
In the whole library?
Yes.

Years later, she fell in love. She wrote his name on the inside of her pencil case. Hoping he might ask to borrow a pen so she could be found out.

In the yard of a house where she lived, there was a large oak tree carved with the initials of each boy she had ever kissed. She put a cross next to the letters F.P. and noticed with a quiet wonder that he shared the same initials as The Frog Prince.

She loved only him.

Like Rapunzel, she grew her hair longer than anyone she knew and for nearly a whole summer, she slept and slept and slept. She stayed inside until her skin turned a powder white against her blood red lips. Each day was spent living and breathing and longing for twisted paths and murderous wolves.

You're living in a fantasy, her mother said.
You need to wake up, her boyfriend told her.

But all she could think about was the boy who was now just an inscription inside a pencil case and two crooked letters carved into an old oak tree.

And the fairy tale his lips once left on the ashen surface of her skin.

A Letter

It was beautifully worded
    and painfully read;
    the things that were written,
    were those never said.

His lies were my comfort,
    but the truth I was owed—
    I so wanted to know it,
    now I wish not to know.

Unrequited

The sun above;
    a stringless kite,
    her tendril fingers
    reach toward.

Her eyes, like flowers,
    close at night,
    and the moon is sad
    to be ignored.

Concentric Circles

Aging is a euphemism for dying, and the age of a tree can only be counted by its rings, once felled.

Sometimes I feel there are so many rings inside me—and if anyone were to look, they would see I have lived and died many times over, each time shedding my leaves bare with the hope of renewal—the desire to be reborn.

Like concentric circles that spill outwards across the water—I wish I could wear my rings on the surface and feel less ashamed of them. Or better yet, to be completely stripped and baptized—my lines vanishing like a newly pressed garment, a still pond.

Edgar's Gift

Anything and everything,
    the two almost the same—
    everything says, have it all;
    anything, one to claim.

If I say, I'd give you everything,
    we know it can never be,
    but I will give you anything—
    I just hope that thing is me.

PRETEXT

Our love—a dead star
    to the world it burns brightly—

    But it died long ago.

Living a Lie

Thoughts that she
    cannot unthink;
    a life that she
    cannot unlive.

Skipping stones
    to watch them sink;
    she envies how
    they easily.

Sorrow wraps her
    like a scarf;
    waiting for a
    small reprieve—
    falling in and out
    of love.

Soundtracks

He once told me about his love for lyrics. How the words spoke to him like poetry.

I would often wonder about his playlist and the ghosts who lived there. The faces he saw and the voices he heard. The soundtrack to a thousand tragic endings, real or imagined.

The first time I saw him, I noticed how haunted his eyes were. And I was drawn to him, in the way a melody draws a crowd to the dance floor. Pulled by invisible strings.

Now I wonder if I am one of those ghosts—if I am somewhere, drifting between those notes. I hope I am. I hope whenever my song plays, I am there, whispering in his ear.

A Winter Song

She was the song,
    in a chorus—unheard.
    You were the summer
    in her winter of verse.

Yours was the melody
    she wanted to learn;
    it clung to her lips,
    in silence it yearned.

It seems as though now,
    you forgot every word;
    in a field full of flowers,
    she was the first.

There once was a song
    you reminded her of—
    she no longer longs,
    yet she still loves.

Two Fishermen

A girl came upon a fisherman at the water's edge and watched as he cast his net into the wide, open sea. On closer inspection, she noticed how all the knots that usually held a net together were unknotted.

"Why do you throw a knotless net into the water?" she asked.

"I want to catch all fish in the ocean," he replied. "But there are none I wish to keep."

She walked on a little further and came across another fisherman, holding a simple line. She studied him quietly as he reeled his catch in, before returning it to the water. After he repeated this several times, the girl asked him, "Why do you catch them just to throw them back?"

"There is only one fish I want to catch and so, no other holds my interest."

Shipwrecks

The wild seas for
    which she longed,
    lay far beyond
    the shore.

The shipwreck that
    her lips had sung,
    meant she never
    left at all.

It wasn't 'til
    the tide had won,
    that she learned
    it could not hurt her.

It was the furthest
    she had gone—
    and she never went
    much further.

An Artist in Love

I drew him in my world;
    I write him in my lines,
    I want to be his girl,
    he was never meant as mine.

I drew him in my world;
    He is always on my mind;
    I draw his every line.
    It hurts when he's unkind.

I drew him in my world;
    I draw him all the time,
    but I don't know where
    to draw the line.

False Hope

I don't know if I want you, he says. But I do know I don't want anyone else to have you.

It wasn't good enough, I knew that. Honestly I did. In my mind it was crystal clear. My heart however, was having a serious case of selective hearing. All it heard was, *I don't want anyone else to have you.* And within that—was a glimmer of hope, a spark of optimism.

A Cautionary Tale

There is a girl who never returns her library books. Don't give her your heart—it is unlikely you will ever see it again.

Afterthought

Thoughts I think of presently,
 will come and go with ease—
 while thoughts of you, from long before,
 have yet to make their leave.

The memory of you and I,
 still finds me here and now;
 tomorrow has arrived and gone—
 yet your voice to me, resounds.

For if my present were an echo of,
 a past I can't forget—

Then these thoughts are just
 an afterthought—
 and I am always in its debt.

GROUNDED

The little birds
    who dream of flight;
    who gaze into
    the starry night.

Their tired wings
    fold down and up;
    they try their best
    but it is not enough.

The Very Thing

I often wonder why we want so much, to give others the very thing that we were denied. The mother working tirelessly to provide her child with an education; the little boy who was bullied in school and is now a Nobel Prize-winning advocate for peace. The author who writes happy endings for the characters in her book.

Forewarned

If a boy ever says, you remind me of someone—don't fall in love with him. You will never be anything more than second best.

MIXED MESSAGES

The questions you had never asked
  were things you were afraid to know;
  everything that has come to pass,
  you've made them all up on your own.

There are many words you never said,
  that others dreamed you someday would;
  each of us for all our days—
  will live our lives misunderstood.

Masquerade

As a writer, there is an inclination to step inside someone else's shoes, to get under their skin and see the world through their eyes. In many such scenarios, I have slipped into these roles with the greatest of ease—then out again with the same dexterity.

That was until I found myself in character, playing the girl who falls in love with you. It was then the line between fantasy and reality were so blurred that I no longer knew who I was.

Yet, there was clearly a point when my role was well and truly over. When I had gone above and beyond the required word count. Where I had exhausted every new angle or approach there was to writing our story.

I know it's over, I really do. I know it has been for quite some time. It's over, yet my heart still feels you. You are a memory to me now, but my mind still thinks of you. What we had was finished long ago—yet the words will not stop flowing.

Change of Heart

You were faultless
    I was flawed,

I was lesser
    yet you
    gave more.

Now with time,
    I find you
    on my mind—

Perhaps I loved you,
    after all.

Reasons

I wish I knew why he left. What his reasons were. Why he changed his mind.

For all these years, I have turned it over in my head—all the possibilities—yet none of them make any sense.

And then I think, perhaps it was because he never loved me. But that makes the least sense of all.

All There Was

My greatest lesson learnt,
    you were mine until you weren't.

It was you who taught me so,
    the grace in letting go.

The time we had was all—
    there was not a moment more.

Pen Portrait

She doesn't keep time,
    so she stopped wearing watches.

Her promise won't bind,
    so no one holds her to them.

She lives in the past,
    so her present never catches—

Her thoughts do not last,
    so her pen must tattoo them.

Musical Chairs

When the music stood still, I was standing at an empty chair.

I could feel you smiling behind me. (We sense these things while dreaming.)

Your hands were on my shoulders, your kisses against my neck.

Then from somewhere, the music of a piano as she sings to Mozart, no one will ever know me the way you do.

TELL ME

Tell me if you ever cared,
    if a single thought
    for me was spared.

Tell me when you lie in bed,
    do you think of something
    I once said.

Tell me if you hurt at all,
    when someone says
    my name with yours.

It may have been so long ago,
    but I would give
    the world to know.

Beach Ball

Do you know that feeling? When it's like you've lost something but can't remember what it was. It's as though you're trying so desperately to think of a word but it won't come to you. You've said it a thousand times before and it was always there—right where you left it. But now you can't recall it. You try and try to make it appear and it almost does, but it never does.

There are times when I think it could surface—when I sense it at the tip of my tongue. When I feel it struggling to burst from my chest like a beach ball that can only be held beneath the water for so long.

I can feel it stirring each time someone hurts me. When I smile at a stranger and they don't smile back. When I trust someone with a secret and they betray me. When someone I admire tells me I am not good enough.

I don't know what it is or what I have lost. But I know it was important, I know it once made me happy.

Amends

I wonder if there will be a morning when you'll wake up missing me. That some incident in your life would have finally taught you the value of my worth. And you will feel a surge of longing, when you remember how I was good to you.

When this day comes I hope you will look for me. I hope you will look with the kind of conviction I'd always hoped for, but never had from you. Because I want to be found. And I hope it will be you—who finds me.

The Most

You may not know
      the reason why,
      for a time
      I wasn't I.

There was a man
      who came and went,
      on him every breath
      was spent.

I'm sorry I forgot
      all else—
      it was the most
      I ever felt.

History

In the beginning, I wrote to you and you wrote back. For the first time, I had something worth writing about.

Then somewhere during our correspondence, I deviated—and instead of writing to you, I began writing for you. There was so much to say, things I couldn't tell you and I sensed it was important to put them down somewhere. For inherently, mankind is compelled to record their greatest moments in history and you were mine.

I don't write to you anymore. Nor do I write for you. But I do write—and every word still aches for you.

The Dream

I saw a dream
    long lost to me,
    in search of
    another's waking.

It found a shoreline
    far away
    as the day—
    as my heart,
    was breaking.

And I sighed and wept
    for what could not be—
    and for all that could
    have been,

For every hope
    and every prayer
    long drowned
    beneath the sea.

I fell to sleep
    alone that night,
    to the sound
    of a distant call.

The faintest whisper
    of good-bye—
    and the dream
    was mine, no more.

WISHING STARS

I still search
        for you in crowds,
        in empty fields
        and soaring clouds.

In city lights
        and passing cars,
        on winding roads
        and wishing stars.

I wonder where
        you could be now,
        for years I've not said
        your name out loud.

And longer since
        I called you mine—
        time has passed
        for you and I.

Yet I have learned
        to live without,
        I do not mind—
        I still love you anyhow.

Forever for Now

Stretching out from here to then,
    days before us,
    came and went.

Someday we will meet again,
    for now the end—
    of days on end.

Nostalgia for Today

Do you remember what you once said to me?

One day you will be nostalgic for today.

At the time, I couldn't begin to conceive a future without you—I believed with all my heart we were destined for each other. And in the back of my mind, I always knew I'd feel nostalgic for a moment we shared or a memory we created—but not once, not even for a second—did I imagine it was you I would be nostalgic for.

Poker Face

There was a time I would tell you,
    of all that ached inside;
    the things I held so sacred,
    to all the world I'd hide.

But they became your weapons,
    and slowly I have learnt,
    the less that is said, the better—
    the lesser I'll be hurt.

Of all you've used against me,
    the worst has been my words.

There are things I'll never tell you,
    and it is sad to think it so;
    the more you come to know me—
    the less of me you'll know.

CROSSWORDS

I write to bring you closer. To imagine your fingers trailing the curve of my spine. To recall how the span of your hands were exactly the width of my hips. And how our bodies would fall into each other like words on a crossword puzzle. I write for the raw ache in my bones when the ink seeps into paper—for the bittersweet sorrow that comes from bringing you back.

Forget Me Not

The choice was once
    your choosing,
    before losing
    became my loss.
    I was there in
    your forgetting—
    until I was forgot.

Melancholy Skies

Three summers passed
    of sun-drenched dreams,
    of snow white clouds
    and you and me.

The warmth of love,
    all summer long,
    through winter's chill
    we'd carry on.

Each season's end
    began anew,
    until the last—
    I shared with you.

They gave us years,
    though many ago;
    the spring cries tears—
    the winter, snow.

The Poet

Why do you write? he asked.

So I can take my love for you and give it to the world, I reply.

Because you won't take it from me.

Almost

Do you see
    how I love him true—
    it could have been you.

As for you
    and your love for she—
    it could have been me.

But we were a maybe,
    and never a must—
    when it should have been us.

HE'S FORGOTTEN

Time is to wound
        like wound is to suture,
        when she was his past
        and he is her future.

Perfect

He said to me "You're perfect,
    and I want you to be mine."
    But I felt I wasn't worthy
    and to be perfect, I'll need time.

I knew it would be worth it,
    I could be better if I tried,
    then he got tired of waiting—
    and I watched my chance go by.

Minefield

If you know a boy with eyes of quiet wonderment, who smiles often and speaks rarely—someone who pays the same respect to words as he would a minefield—who thinks deeply and is endearingly sad—please do not give your heart to him. Even when he gently pleads with you—or clutches your hand with grave earnest—no matter how he tries to convince you, please turn him away. You don't know him like I know him. You can't love him like I do.

A Sad Farewell

For all the time I've known you,
  to the present—now our past;
  I know never to forget you;
  though regret still pains my heart.

Had I known, I would not have left you,
  alone beneath those stars,
  on the night when I last saw you,
  not knowing it was the last.

REGRETS

Timing is irrelevant when two people are meant for each other. It's what I once believed.

But we met during a time when I was such a mess, when I still had so much to figure out. How could I have known how crucial every word, every action was or how losing you would be something I would always regret?

If only you could have met me now, how different it would be. How much I have changed. How I have grown. I learned so much from all the mistakes I made with you. I just wish I had made them with someone else.

ODE TO SORROW

Her eyes, a closed book,
    her heart, a locked door;
    she writes melancholy
    like she's lived it before.

She once loved in a way,
    you could not understand;
    he left her in pieces
    and a pen in her hand.

The ode to her sorrow
    in the life she has led—
    her scratches on paper,
    the words they have bled.

Remembering You

The day you left, I went through all my old journals, frantically looking for the first mention of you. Searching for any details I can no longer recall—any morsel of information that may have been lost to my subconscious. The memory of you is fading, a little at a time, and I can feel myself forgetting. I don't want to forget.

Love's Paradox

There is a tide that rolls away,
    I want to make it stay.

A borrowed book sits on my shelf,
    I want it for myself.

There are two old hands
    that move this clock,
    I want to make them stop.

There is a love you sold to me,
    I keep it under lock—
    and yet you hold the key.

A Ghost

His voice in this room,
    like shadows on walls;
    I imagine him on
    the other side of the door.

His voice, his hands, his touch,
    at the start, the end,
    and in the middle.

Strange how it mattered so much,
    when now it matters
    so little.

Losing You

I used to think I couldn't go a day without your smile. Without telling you things and hearing your voice back.

Then, that day arrived and it was so damn hard but the next was harder. I knew with a sinking feeling it was going to get worse, and I wasn't going to be okay for a very long time.

Because losing someone isn't an occasion or an event. It doesn't just happen once. It happens over and over again. I lose you every time I pick up your favorite coffee mug; whenever that one song plays on the radio, or when I discover your old t-shirt at the bottom of my laundry pile.

I lose you every time I think of kissing you, holding you, or wanting you. I go to bed at night and lose you, when I wish I could tell you about my day. And in the morning, when I wake and reach for the empty space across the sheets, I begin to lose you all over again.

The End

"I don't know what to say," he said.

"It's okay," she replied, "I know what we are—
and I know what we're not."

Encore

Excerpts from
Love & Misadventure

Also by Lang Leav

*Available where all
good books are sold*

Angels

It happens like this. One day you meet someone and for some inexplicable reason, you feel more connected to this stranger than anyone else—closer to them than your closest family. Perhaps because this person carries an angel within them—one sent to you for some higher purpose, to teach you an important lesson or to keep you safe during a perilous time. What you must do is trust in them—even if they come hand in hand with pain or suffering—the reason for their presence will become clear in due time.

Though here is a word of warning—you may grow to love this person but remember they are not yours to keep. Their purpose isn't to save you but to show you how to save yourself. And once this is fulfilled, the halo lifts and the angel leaves their body as the person exits your life. They will be a stranger to you once more.

. . . .

It's so dark right now, I can't see any light around me.
That's because the light is coming from you. You can't see it but everyone else can.

Souls

When two souls fall in love, there is nothing else but the yearning to be close to the other. The presence that is felt through a hand held, a voice heard, or a smile seen.

Souls do not have calendars or clocks, nor do they understand the notion of time or distance. They only know it feels right to be with one another.

This is the reason why you miss someone so much when they are not there—even if they are only in the very next room. Your soul only feels their absence—it doesn't realize the separation is temporary.

. . . .

Can I ask you something?
Anything.
Why is it every time we say good night, it feels like good-bye?

A Dream

As the Earth began spinning faster and faster, we floated upwards, hands locked tightly together, eyes sad and bewildered. We watched as our faces grew younger and realized the Earth was spinning in reverse, moving us backwards in time.

Then we reached a point where I no longer knew who you were and I was grasping the hands of a stranger. But I didn't let go. And neither did you.

. . . .

I had my first dream about you last night.
Really? She smiles. What was it about?
I don't remember exactly, but the whole time I was dreaming, I knew you were mine.

Rogue Planets

As a kid, I would count backwards from ten and imagine at one, there would be an explosion—perhaps caused by a rogue planet crashing into Earth or some other major catastrophe. When nothing happened, I'd feel relieved and at the same time, a little disappointed.

I think of you at ten; the first time I saw you. Your smile at nine and how it lit up something inside me I had thought long dead. Your lips at eight pressed against mine and at seven, your warm breath in my ear and your hands everywhere. You tell me you love me at six and at five we have our first real fight. At four we have our second and three, our third. At two you tell me you can't go on any longer and then at one, you ask me to stay.

And I am relieved, so relieved—and a little disappointed.

Sea of Strangers

In a sea of strangers,
    you've longed to know me.
    Your life spent sailing
    to my shores.

The arms that yearn
    to someday hold me,
    will ache beneath
    the heavy oars.

Please take your time
    and take it slowly;
    as all you do
    will run its course.

And nothing else
    can take what only—
    was always meant
    as solely yours.

CLOSURE

Like time suspended,
    a wound unmended—
    you and I.

We had no ending,
    no said good-bye.

For all my life,
    I'll wonder why.

Acknowledgments

Thank you to my agent, Al Zuckerman, for his invaluable guidance and wonderful support.

To Kirsty Melville and her passionate team at Andrews McMeel, for sending my books out into the world.

To all the amazing people I have had the pleasure of meeting on my book tours (you know who you are), thank you for working so tirelessly behind the scenes and for making me feel so welcome on my visits.

To my family and friends, it goes without saying that I wouldn't be here without your love and encouragement.

To Ollie Faudet, who likes cows and makes me laugh.

And last, but definitely not least—a very special thank you to all of my beautiful readers. Your unwavering support and kind words inspire me every day.

About the Author

The work of poet and artist Lang Leav swings between the whimsical and woeful, expressing a complexity beneath its childlike facade.

Lang is a recipient of the Qantas Spirit of Youth Award and a prestigious Churchill Fellowship.

Her artwork is exhibited internationally and she was selected to take part in the landmark Playboy Redux show curated by the Andy Warhol Museum.

She currently lives with her partner and collaborator, Michael, in a little house by the sea.

INDEX

ENCORE   219

235

POSTED POEMS

Posted Poems is a unique postal service that allows you to send your favorite Lang Leav poem to anyone, anywhere in the world. All poems are printed on heavyweight art paper and encased in a beautiful string-tie envelope. To send a Posted Poem to someone special visit: langleav.com/postedpoems

Love & Misadventure

Love & Misadventure

Written & Illustrated by

L A N G   L E A V

Andrews McMeel
PUBLISHING®

Andrews McMeel Publishing
a division of Andrews McMeel Universal
1130 Walnut Street, Kansas City, Missouri 64106

www.andrewsmcmeel.com

www.langleav.com

ISBN: 978-1-4494-5614-6

Library of Congress Control Number: 2013947184

This book is a work of fiction. Names, characters, places, and
incidents either are products of the author's imagination or are
used fictitiously. Any resemblance to actual events or locales or
persons, living or dead, is entirely coincidental.

ATTENTION: SCHOOLS AND BUSINESSES
Andrews McMeel books are available at quantity discounts
with bulk purchase for educational, business, or sales
promotional use. For information, please e-mail the
Andrews McMeel Publishing Special Sales Department:
specialsales@amuniversal.com.

For Michael

The half of this book—
the whole of my heart.

A Dedication

She lends her pen,
    to thoughts of him,
    that flow from it,
    in her solitary.

For she is his poet,
    And he is her poetry.

Part I

MISADVENTURE

A Toast!

To new beginnings,
    in fear and faith
    and all it tinges.

To love is a dare,
    when hope and despair,
    are gates upon it hinges.

Xs and Os

Love is a game
    of tic-tac-toe,
    constantly waiting,
    for the next x or o.

A Dangerous Recipe

To love him
    is something,
    I hold highly
    suspicious.

Like having something,
    so very delicious—
    then being told,
    to do the dishes.

Just Friends

I know that I don't own you,
    and perhaps I never will,
    so my anger when you're with her,
    I have no right to feel.

I know that you don't owe me,
    and I shouldn't ask for more;
    I shouldn't feel so let down,
    all the times when you don't call.

What I feel—I shouldn't show you,
    so when you're around I won't;
    I know I've no right to feel it—
    but it doesn't mean I don't.

When Ignorance Is Bliss

I deplore,
    being ignored.

For—

I am not a bore!

But it's perplexingly sweet,
    and quite sexy too—
      to be ignored,
      ignored by you.

HEART ON THE LINE

Love is good,
    it is never bad—
    but it will drive you mad!

When it is given to you,
    in dribs and drabs.

Sea of Strangers

In a sea of strangers,
　　you've longed to know me.
　　Your life spent sailing
　　to my shores.

The arms that yearn
　　to someday hold me,
　　will ache beneath
　　the heavy oars.

Please take your time
　　and take it slowly;
　　as all you do
　　will run its course.

And nothing else
　　can take what only—
　　was always meant
　　as solely yours.

ART AND BOOKS

Without a doubt,
    I must read,
    all the books
    I've read about.

See the artworks
    hung on hooks,
    that I have only,
    seen in books.

A Voyage

To be guided
  nor misguided
  in love,
  nor brokenhearted.

But to sail in waters—
  uncharted.

A Thank-You Note

You have said
    all the things
    I need to hear
    before I knew
    I needed to hear them.

To be unafraid
    of all the things
    I used to fear,
    before I knew
    I shouldn't fear them.

An Endearing Trait

The scatterbrain,
    is a little like,
    the patter of rain.

Neither here,
    nor there,
    but everywhere.

His Word

I am not,
    just a notch
    on his belt.

What he feels for me,
    he's never felt.

I am a word
    he has heard
    but has never seen
    for himself.

Yet he wants to know,
    how that word
    is spelt.

A Well-Dressed Man

His charm
    will disarm;
    his smile,
    in style;
    his fashion,
    in passion;
    his words,
    his flirt,
    his tie
    from his shirt,
    to my wrists—
    his kiss!
    his kiss!
    his kiss!

A Stranger

There is a love I reminisce,
    like a seed
    I've never sown.

Of lips that I am yet to kiss,
    and eyes
    not met my own.

Hands that wrap around my wrists,
    and arms
    that feel like home.

I wonder how it is I miss,
    these things
    I've never known.

Wallflower

Shrinking in a corner,
    pressed into the wall;
    do they know I'm present,
    am I here at all?

Is there a written rule book,
    that tells you how to be—
    all the right things to talk about—
    that everyone has but me?

Slowly I am withering—
    a flower deprived of sun;
    longing to belong to—
    somewhere or someone.

A Rollercoaster

You will find him in
    my highs and lows;
    in my mind,
    he'll to and fro.

He's the tallest person,
    that I know—
    and so he keeps me,
    on my toes.

His Cause and Effect

He makes me turn,
>he makes me toss;
>his words mean mine
>are at a loss.

He makes me blush!

He makes me want
>to brush and floss.

Lost and Found

A sunken chest,
    on the ocean ground,
    to never be found
    was where he found me.

There he stirred,
    my every thought,
    my every word,
    so gently, so profoundly.

Now I am kept,
    from dreams I dreamt,
    when once I slept,
    so soundly.

Afraid to Love

I turn away
    and close my heart—
    to the promise of love
    that is luring.

For the past has taught
    to not be caught,
    in what is not
    worth pursuing—

To never do
    the things I've done
    that once had led
    to my undoing.

The Wanderer

What is she like?
    I was told—
    she is a
    melancholy soul.

She is like
    the sun to night;
    a momentary gold.

A star when dimmed
    by dawning light;
    the flicker of
    a candle blown.

A lonely kite
    lost in flight—
    someone once
    had flown.

Part 2

THE CIRCUS OF SORROWS

Circus Town

From a city so bright
    to a strange little town;
    on a carousel spinning,
    around and around.

The dizzying height,
    of the stars from the ground.

The world all alight—
    with his sights, his sounds.

A Timeline

You and I
     against a rule,
     set for us by time.

A marker drawn
     to show our end,
     etched into its line.

The briefest moment
     shared with you—
     the longest
     on my mind.

In Two Parts

You come and go so easily,
    your life is as you knew—
    while mine is split in two.

How I envy so the half of me,
    who lived before love's due,
    who was yet to know of you.

A Bad Day

When thoughts of all but one,
    are those I am keeping.

When sore though there is none,
    for whom I am weeping.

A curtain drawn before the sun,
    and I wish to go on sleeping.

Rogue Planets

As a kid, I would count backwards from ten and imagine at one, there would be an explosion—perhaps caused by a rogue planet crashing into Earth or some other major catastrophe. When nothing happened, I'd feel relieved and at the same time, a little disappointed.

I think of you at ten; the first time I saw you. Your smile at nine and how it lit up something inside me I had thought long dead. Your lips at eight pressed against mine and at seven, your warm breath in my ear and your hands everywhere. You tell me you love me at six and at five we have our first real fight. At four we have our second and three, our third. At two you tell me you can't go on any longer and then at one, you ask me to stay.

And I am relieved, so relieved—and a little disappointed.

Closure

Like time suspended,
    a wound unmended—
    you and I.

We had no ending,
    no said good-bye.

For all my life,
    I'll wonder why.

A QUESTION

It was a question I had worn on my lips for days—like a loose thread on my favorite sweater I couldn't resist pulling—despite knowing it could all unravel around me.

"Do you love me?" I ask.

In your hesitation I found my answer.

A Way Out

Do you know what it is like,
    to lie in bed awake;
    with thoughts to haunt
    you every night,
    of all your past mistakes.

Knowing sleep will set it right—
    if you were not to wake.

Lost Things

Do you know when you've lost something—like your favorite T-shirt or a set of keys—and while looking for it, you come across something else you once missed but have long since forgotten? Well whatever it was, there was a point where you decided to stop searching, maybe because it was no longer required or a new replacement was found. It is almost as if it never existed in the first place—until that moment of rediscovery, a flash of recognition.

Everyone has one—an inventory of lost things waiting to be found. Yearning to be acknowledged for the worth they once held in your life.

I think this is where I belong—among all your other lost things. A crumpled note at the bottom of a drawer or an old photograph pressed between the pages of a book. I hope someday you will find me and remember what I once meant to you.

A Betrayal

I cannot undo
    what I have done;
    I can't un-sing
    a song that's sung.

And the saddest thing
    about my regret—

I can't forgive me,
    and you can't forget.

After You

If I wrote it in a book,
    could I shelve it?

If I told of what you took,
    would that help it?

If I will it,
    can I un-feel it,
    now I've felt it?

A Reverie

A dusty room,
    a window chair,
    unseeing eyes
    that gaze into
    the montage of
    a love affair.

A carousel
    of memories,
    spinning round
    into a blur.

Her mind is now
    a fairground ride—
    she wonders if
    you think of her.

Letting Him Go

There is a particular kind of suffering to be experienced when you love something greater than yourself. A tender sacrifice.

Like the pained silence felt in the lost song of a mermaid; or the bent and broken feet of a dancing ballerina. It is in every considered step I am taking in the opposite direction of you.

The Things We Hide

And so,
    I have put away
    the photographs,
    every trace of you
    I know.

The things that seem
    to matter less,
    are the ones
    we put on show.

Love Lost

There is one who you belong to,
    whose love—there is no song for.
    And though you know it's wrongful,
    there is someone else you long for.

Your heart was once a vessel,
    it was filled up to the brim;
    until the day he left you,
    now everything sings of him.

Of the two who came to love you,
    to one, your heart you gave.
    He lives in stars above you—
    in the love who came and stayed.

Time Travelers

In all our wrongs,
    I want to write him,
    in a time where
    I can find him.

Before the tears
    that tore us.

When our history was
    before us.

A Small Consolation

Everything that we once were,
  is now a sad and lonely verse.

When once I had so much to say,
  I am now bereft of words.

Sometimes it is the order of things,
  that make them seem much worse.

It's not as if you would have stayed,
  if I hadn't left you first.

An Impossible Task

To try
    or untry
    to forget you not,
    may be related
    somewhat—

To tying,
    then trying
    to untie,
    a complicated
    knot.

The Keeper

You were like a dream,
    I wish I hadn't
    slept through.

Within it I fell deeper,
    than your heart would
    care to let you.

I thought you were a keeper,
    I wish I could
    have kept you.

Sad Songs

Once there was a boy who couldn't speak but owned a music box that held every song in all the world. One day he met a girl who had never heard a single melody in her entire life and so he played her his favorite song. He watched while her face lit up with wonder as the music filled the sky and the poetry of lyrics moved her in a way she had never felt before.

He would play his songs for her day after day and she would sit by him quietly—never seeming to mind that he could only speak to her through song. She loved everything he played for her, but of them all—she loved the sad songs best. So he began to play them more and more until eventually, sad songs were all she would hear.

One day, he noticed it had been a very long time since her last smile. When he asked her why, she took both his hands in hers and kissed them warmly. She thanked him for his gift of music and poetry but above all else—for showing her sadness because she had known neither of these things before him. But it was now time for her to go away—to find someone who could show her what happiness was.

. . . .

Do you remember the song that was playing the night we met?
No, but I remember every song I have heard since you left.

Jealousy

It was the way
　　you spoke about her.

With animosity, regret, disdain
　　and underneath it all—
　　just a hint of pride.

Waking without You

Every song that sings of him,
    from every heart
    heard breaking.

I sing along in dreams of him,
    I cling to—
    when I start waking.

That Day

I remember our highs in hues,
    like the color of his eyes
    as the sun was setting;
    the pale of his hands in mine,
    and the blue of his smile.

I remember our sorrows in shades,
    like the gray of the shadows,
    which loomed that day,
    and the white in his lie
    when he promised to stay.

THE GIRL HE LOVES

There was a man who I once knew,
    for me there was no other.
    The closer to loving me he grew,
    the more he would grow further.

I tried to love him as his friend,
    then to love him as his lover;
    but he never loved me in the end—
    his heart was for another.

A Lover's Past

The turbulent turns
    and the tides
    that twist them.

When what they once were,
    was how she
    had wished them.

And all the joys he brought her,
    how she could
    list them.

In time she will learn,
    not to
    miss them.

Beauty's Curse

Her bow is drawn
      to worlds of dark;
      where arrows spring
      and miss their mark.

She'll turn their heads—
      but not their hearts.

DEAD BUTTERFLIES

I sometimes think about the fragility of glass—of broken shards tearing against soft skin. When in truth, it is the transparency that kills you. The pain of seeing through to something you can never quite touch.

For years I've kept you in secret, behind a glass screen. I've watched helplessly as day after day, your new girlfriend becomes your wife and then later, the mother of your children. Then realizing the irony in thinking you were the one under glass when in fact it has been me—a pinned butterfly—static and unmoving, watching while your other life unfolds.

Wishful Thinking

You say that you are over me,
    my heart—
    it skips,
    it sinks.

I see you now with someone new,
    I stare,
    I stare,
    I blink.

Someday I'll be over you,
    I know,
    I know—
    I think.

A Heavy Heart

All you have done,
    I had hoped to pardon.

When the death of love
      was slow for me—
      for you was sudden.

Now the years go by,
     and my heart
     has hardened.

Saving You

The darkness takes him over,
    the sickness pulls him in;
    his eyes—a blown-out candle;
    I wish to go with him.

Sometimes I see a flicker—
    a light that shone from them;
    I hold him to me tightly,
    before he's gone again.

AN ANSWER

To choose from
　　there were many;
　　among them,
　　there were some.

And of those I loved you,
　　more than any—
　　but not as much
　　as one.

Swan Song

Her heart is played
        like well-worn strings;
        in her eyes,
        the sadness sings—
        of one who was destined
        for better things.

Part 3
LOVE

First Love

Before I fell
       in love with words,
       with setting skies
       and singing birds—
       it was you I fell
       in love with first.

He and I

When words run dry,
    he does not try,
    nor do I.

We are on par.

He just is,
    I just am,
    and we just are.

Sundays with Michael

I hold my breath and count to ten,
    I stand and sit, then stand again.
    I cross and then uncross my legs,
    the planes are flying overhead.

The dial turns with every twist,
    around the watch, around his wrist.
    Resting there with pen in hand,
    who could ever understand?

The way he writes of all I dream,
    things kind yet cruel and in-between,
    where underneath those twisted trees,
    a pretty girl fallen to her knees.

Who could know the world we've spun?
    I shrug my shoulders and hold my tongue.
    I hold my breath and count to ten,
    I stand and sit, then stand again.

Mornings with You

I slowly wake
    as day is dawning,
    to fingertips
    and lips imploring.

The sheets against my skin,
    he says,
    like wrapping paper
    on Christmas morning.

Soul Mates

I don't know how you are so familiar to me—or why it feels less like I am getting to know you and more as though I am remembering who you are. How every smile, every whisper brings me closer to the impossible conclusion that I have known you before, I have loved you before—in another time, a different place—some other existence.

A Fairy Tale

Start of spring;
    heart in bloom;
    our whisperings
    in sunlit rooms.

Summer was felt
    a little more;
    in autumn I
    began to fall.

When winter came
    with all its white,
    you were mine
    to kiss goodnight.

Always

You were you,
    and I was I;
    we were two
    before our time.

I was yours
    before I knew,
    and you have always
    been mine too.

A Dream

As the Earth began spinning faster and faster, we floated upwards, hands locked tightly together, eyes sad and bewildered. We watched as our faces grew younger and realized the Earth was spinning in reverse, moving us backwards in time.

Then we reached a point where I no longer knew who you were and I was grasping the hands of a stranger. But I didn't let go. And neither did you.

. . . .

I had my first dream about you last night.
Really? She smiles. What was it about?
I don't remember exactly, but the whole time I was dreaming, I knew you were mine.

Before There Was You

When I used to look above,
    all I saw was sky;
    and every song
    that I would sing,
    I sung not knowing why.

All I thought and all I felt,
    was only just because,
    never was it ever you—
    until it was all there was.

Beautiful

Your hand reaches for mine.
    We kiss tentatively, passionately
    and then, tenderly.

You brush my hair away from my face.
    "You're beautiful."
    I wrinkle my nose in protest.
    "You are."

All or Nothing

If you love me
    for what you see,
    only your eyes would be
    in love with me.

If you love me
    for what you've heard,
    then you would love me
    for my words.

If you love
    my heart and mind,
    then you would love me,
    for all that I'm.

But if you don't love
    my every flaw,
    then you mustn't love me—
    not at all.

Some Time Out

The time may not
      be prime for us,
      though you are
      a special person.

We may be just
      two different clocks,
      that do not tock,
      in unison.

Souls

When two souls fall in love, there is nothing else but the yearning to be close to the other. The presence that is felt through a hand held, a voice heard, or a smile seen.

Souls do not have calendars or clocks, nor do they understand the notion of time or distance. They only know it feels right to be with one another.

This is the reason why you miss someone so much when they are not there—even if they are only in the very next room. Your soul only feels their absence—it doesn't realize the separation is temporary.

. . . .

Can I ask you something?
Anything.
Why is it every time we say good night, it feels like good-bye?

Solo Show

He pulls the thick woolen sweater
    up, over my head.

Little sparks of static
    dance across my skin.

Does it hurt? He says, running his hands
    gently over my warm body.

It is your own little fireworks show,
    I whisper.

The Fear of Losing You

Without meaning to,
    he's disarmed me,
    with kisses that soothe
    and alarm me.

In arms that terrify
    and calm me.

Ebb and Flow

She yearns to learn
     how his tide is turned,
     to understand
     each grain of sand,
     he knows.

To move in rhythm,
     with his ebb and flow.

Written in Traffic

A quiet gladness,
    in the busy sadness;
    inside the final tussle,
    of love and its madness.

Its goodness and badness,
    its hustle and bustle.

Angels

It happens like this. One day you meet someone and for some inexplicable reason, you feel more connected to this stranger than anyone else—closer to them than your closest family. Perhaps because this person carries an angel within them—one sent to you for some higher purpose, to teach you an important lesson or to keep you safe during a perilous time. What you must do is trust in them—even if they come hand in hand with pain or suffering—the reason for their presence will become clear in due time.

Though here is a word of warning—you may grow to love this person but remember they are not yours to keep. Their purpose isn't to save you but to show you how to save yourself. And once this is fulfilled, the halo lifts and the angel leaves their body as the person exits your life. They will be a stranger to you once more.

. . . .

It's so dark right now, I can't see any light around me.
That's because the light is coming from you. You can't see it but everyone else can.

Golden Cage

A bird who hurt her wing,
  now forgotten how to fly.

A song she used to sing,
  but can't remember why.

A breath she caught and kept—
  that left her in a sigh.

It hurts her so to love you,
  but she won't say good-bye.

LOVE LETTERS

Every letter
  that she types,
  every keystroke
  that she strikes—

To spell your name
  again and again—
  is all she ever
  wants to write.

CODEPENDENCY

There is nothing more nice,
    there is nothing much worser;
    than me as your vice
    and you as my versa.

Canyons

Rarely do the words *I love you* precede a question mark—but it is a question nonetheless and your answer to mine was the incarnation of a wish—the fulfillment of a promise.

Somewhere between falling in and out of love, the question spilled from our lips over and over—readily answered with greedy hands and ravenous mouths. It was cautiously whispered on rooftops, as we looked down on terrifying heights and cried out under creased, white sheets in breathless admissions.

Towards good-bye, I asked the question, and your reply was a thoughtless echo as I stood, feeling as though I was shouting meaningless words into an empty canyon—just to hear them repeated back.

. . . .

I love you, he says for the first time.
I turn my body to face his. *Say it again.*
He says it over and over again, pulling me beneath him.

A Time Capsule

This is where,
    I began to care,
    where I was befriended.

This is where,
    my soul was bared,
    where all my rules were bended.

This is where,
    a moment we shared,
    was stolen and expended.

Now this is where,
    this is where,
    this is where we've ended—

Index

About the Author

The work of poet and artist Lang Leav swings between the whimsical and woeful, expressing a complexity beneath its childlike facade.

Lang is a recipient of the Qantas Spirit of Youth Award and a prestigious Churchill Fellowship.

Her artwork is exhibited internationally and she was selected to take part in the landmark Playboy Redux show curated by the Andy Warhol Museum.

She currently lives with her partner and collaborator, Michael, in a little house by the sea.

POSTED POEMS

Posted Poems is a unique postal service that allows you to send your favorite Lang Leav poem to anyone, anywhere in the world. All poems are printed on heavyweight art paper and encased in a beautiful string-tie envelope. To send a Posted Poem to someone special visit: langleav.com/postedpoems